Y0-DLE-487

KALEIDOSCOPE
KIDS BIBLES REIMAGINED

© 2021 kaleidoscope kids, llc

all rights reserved.
no part of this publication may be reproduced, distributed, or transmitted in any form or by any means, including photocopying or other electronic or mechanical method, without prior written permission of kaleidoscope kids, llc except in the case of brief quotations embodied in critical reviews and certain other noncommercial uses permitted by copyright law. for permission requests, please write to us at hello@readkaleidoscope.com.

published in the united states by kaleidoscope kids llc

visit us at www.readkaleidoscope.com

kaleidoscope, *kids bibles reimagined*

library of congress cataloging-in-publication data is available upon request
ISBN
978-1-7360171-8-0

cover art by becca godfrey @becca.godfrey
logo design by morgan carter @bymorgancarter
editing by bethany denton @betdenton

To Courtney, for encouraging
and helping me
every step along the way.
I adore you, buddy!

WELCOME TO KALEIDOSCOPE

First of all, thank you for picking up a copy of Kaleidoscope! We are glad to have you. In the following pages, you'll experience the Bible in a whole new way.

Kaleidoscope was borne from the need to provide a retelling of the Bible for elementary-aged children that is between a "little kid" Bible and an adult translation. In a way, we are the happy medium.

At Kaleidoscope, we are producing single volumes for every book of the Bible. They are designed to read like chapter books, so you'll turn pages and look forward with anticipation to the next volume.

But don't let the fact that we are focused on kids deter you if you are a "big kid!" Good children's books are almost always as good for adults as they are for kids.

Get excited! In the pages that follow, you'll see God's wonderful good news. Our prayer is that his kindness, gentleness, and love will melt our hearts and make us more like Jesus.

The Kaleidoscope Team

Never Deserted is a gift to the church. Both children and adults will love this easily accessible, conversational, and gospel-rich retelling of the book of Numbers. In this volume of Kaleidoscope, we find people who are much like us: grumbling, forgetful, and prone to wander. And we find a God who keeps His people anyway, and who refuses to remove His hand of blessing. Your hearts, and the hearts of your children, will be stirred with affection for Christ who endured the desert for us perfectly, so that we would never be deserted.

-Elizabeth Harwell, author of *The Good Shepherd's Pasture: A Story of Your Baptism* and *The Good King's Feast: An Invitation to the Lord's Table*

A job well done! Daniel does a great job of placing the story of Numbers on a young reader's level. Fun, engaging, and practical, this edition summarizes well the big picture of God's unchanging character and love.

-Courtney Kassner, owner of Crew+Co

The anger of God is difficult to grasp at any age, but *Never Deserted* highlights themes from the book of Numbers that reminds kids (and parents) that God is always motivated by perfect love and will never leave us despite the wrong we do. Teaching kids to understand and appreciate God's Word is what Kaleidoscope does best—*Never Deserted* is another great addition to your family's collection.

-Bailey T. Hurley, author, and friendship coach, @bailey.t.hurley

What a delightful book! Not only is the material contained within theologically sound, but it is presented in an accessible way that the children of the church I serve will devour.

-Les Newsom, Lead Pastor of Christ Presbyterian in Oxford, MS, and co-author of *The Enduring Community: Embracing the Priority of the Church*

Never Deserted is not only beautifully written, but also so fun to read! It allows children to better grasp God's provision and goodness through the experiences and struggles that the Israelites faced. I think that as children read and reflect on how God led His people through the wilderness, they too will learn to trust and love the same God who will lead them. I'm so grateful for this spectacular resource!

-Emma Barnett, Crew+Co

CREATORS

Daniel Hightower is a pastor with Reformed University Fellowship at Jacksonville State University. He earned his degree in Spanish from Troy University and his M.Div. from Beeson Divinity School. He's a husband to Courtney and a dad to four of the best kiddos on Earth—Naomi, Rebekah, Cole, and Sam. When he's not wrestling around with all those wild children of his, you can find him rocking out on the guitar or playing a nerdy board game.

Marlena Sigman is an artist and designer based in Greenville, South Carolina. She earned a fine arts degree in design at Auburn University, and has a deep love for color, shape, and typography. She finds inspiration in thrift stores, historic buildings, newgrass, and classic literature. If she's not creating art, she's traveling or playing with her dog.

TABLE OF CONTENTS

MOSES COUNTS THE PEOPLE   1
   NUMBERS 1

MORE COUNTING, MORE RULES &   5
A BENEDICTION
   NUMBERS 2-6

GOD'S BIG PARTY   11
   NUMBERS 7-9

THE TROUBLE BEGINS   17
   NUMBERS 10-12

A HAPPY DAY TURNED SAD   25
   NUMBERS 13-14:38

CONSEQUENCES & COMMITMENT   31
   NUMBERS 14:39-15:21

HEY, WHO'S IN CHARGE? NUMBERS 16-17:11	37
FAILING THE TEST NUMBERS 20	43
HINTS OF HOPE NUMBERS 21	49
A WIZARD & HIS TALKING DONKEY NUMBERS 22	55
BALAAM SPEAKS GOD'S WORDS NUMBERS 23-24	61
OLD SIN & NEW BEGINNINGS NUMBERS 25-27	67
A TASTE OF THE FUTURE NUMBERS 28-36	71
LAST WORDS: JESUS DEFEATS TEMPTATION MATTHEW 4:1-11	77

INTRODUCTION

It probably won't surprise you that the book of the Bible called Numbers starts with, well...numbers! A whole lot of them. In addition to all the numbers, there are also long lists and instructions repeated over and over. But before we talk about all that, let's remember what's happened in the Bible so far.

Long ago, God chose two very important people named Abraham and Sarah in His plan to rescue the world. Even though they were very old and had no children, God promised that they would have more kids than they could ever count. Abraham and Sarah's kids would be His special people.

Years passed and, sure enough, Abraham and Sarah had a son named Isaac. Isaac had a son named Jacob. And Jacob had a lot of sons. All those sons moved to Egypt and had more kids of their own. But years later, the evil Pharaoh of Egypt made God's people his slaves.

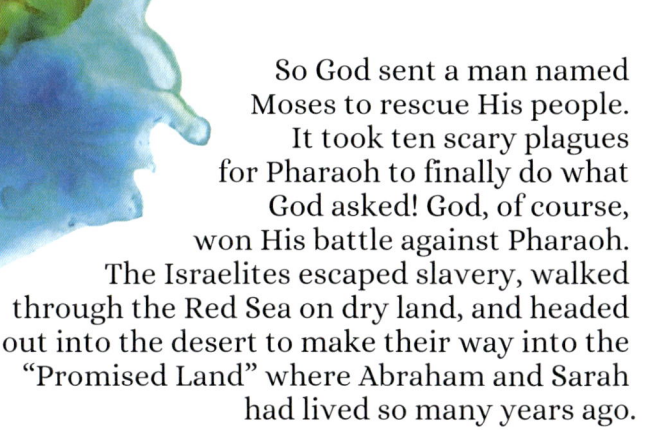

So God sent a man named Moses to rescue His people. It took ten scary plagues for Pharaoh to finally do what God asked! God, of course, won His battle against Pharaoh. The Israelites escaped slavery, walked through the Red Sea on dry land, and headed out into the desert to make their way into the "Promised Land" where Abraham and Sarah had lived so many years ago.

Now, back to Numbers. Have you ever played a board game? If you have, you know that there are usually lots of instructions to go with it—telling you where to put the pieces and cards and dice. There are usually lots of rules to follow too. Numbers is a lot like that. Israel was a real nation now. So, God wanted to tell them how to organize, what to do, and how to live as they made their way through the desert. You'd have one mess of a nation without any rules to live by!

Numbers is not just filled with instructions, though. It's also filled with stories. Most of these stories are about how Israel did not trust God, and how they thought they could live a better life on their own. But even though the people of Israel disobeyed God time and time again, He could not stop loving them. And even though He punished them for their disobedience, He kept protecting them and giving them gift after gift after gift.

That gift-giving God is the same God who loves and protects us now. So are you ready for a great adventure? Let's dive in and see what Numbers teaches us about our great God and His great love for us!

MOSES COUNTS THE PEOPLE

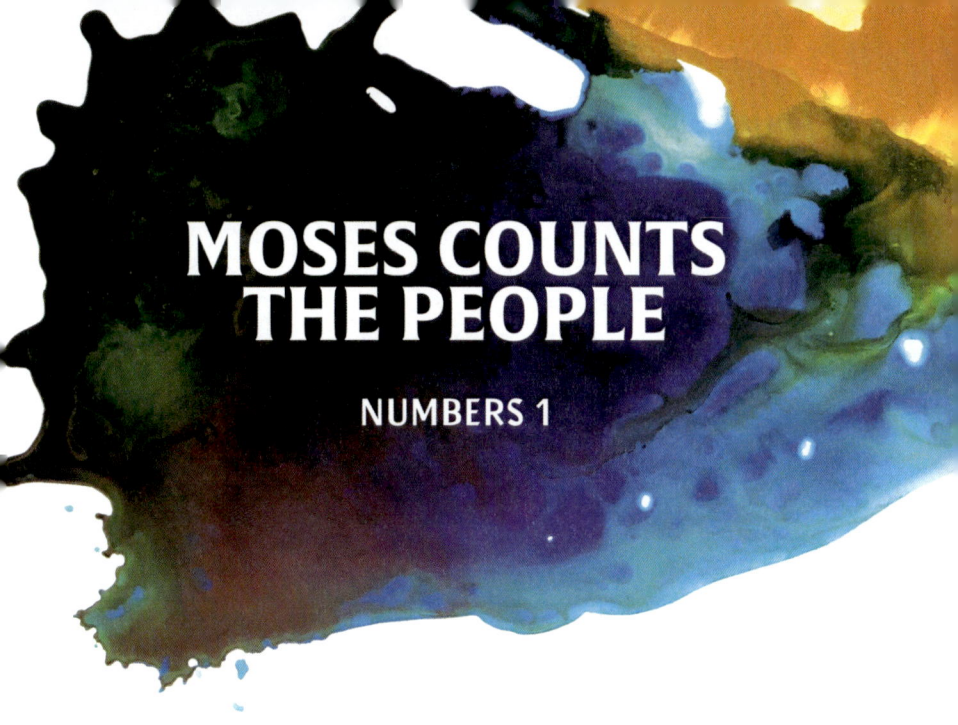

NUMBERS 1

A whole year had passed since God rescued His people from slavery in Egypt. Moses was in the tabernacle when the LORD began speaking to him: "Count all of the men in every family in every neighborhood in every group. Count every man who can fight in a war—20 years old and older." (See Kaleidoscope Corner at the end of this chapter for more on the tabernacle.)

Moses and Aaron needed a lot more fingers to count on for this giant math problem! But, as we'll see throughout the book of Numbers, God had just the right plan for this (and every!) situation.

The LORD said again, "There are so many people. You're going to need help. For this reason, I found a helper from each tribe (like a really big family) that can count for you."

So, that same day, Moses and Aaron got all of God's helpers together, and they started counting and counting...and counting.

From Reuben's tribe: 46,500 men.
From Simeon's tribe: 59,300 men.
From Gad's tribe: 45,650 men.
From Judah's tribe: 74,600 men.
From Issachar's tribe: 54,400 men.
From Zebulun's tribe: 57,400 men.
From Ephraim's tribe: 40,500 men.
From Manasseh's tribe: 32,200 men.
From Benjamin's tribe: 35,400 men.
From Dan's tribe: 62,700 men.
From Asher's tribe: 41,500 men.
From Naphtali's tribe: 53,400 men.

And the grand total: 603,500 men who could fight in a war! (See? Lots of numbers! But behind each one of those numbers was a precious Israelite that God loved with all His heart.)

Now, hold on a second! One of the tribes was missing. Where's Levi's tribe? Well, God had a very special job for them.

God told Moses, "When you count all the people, don't count Levi's tribe. They're going to take care of My tabernacle and everything inside of it. When we get up and walk through the desert, they're in charge of packing everything up and carrying it. And when we find a place to stop, they're in charge of setting the tabernacle back up again. All the other families will live where I tell them, but the Levites need to live near the tabernacle. They'll protect it because it is My special place where I come to meet with My people."

And you know what? The Israelites (which is another name for God's people) obeyed everything God told Moses to do.

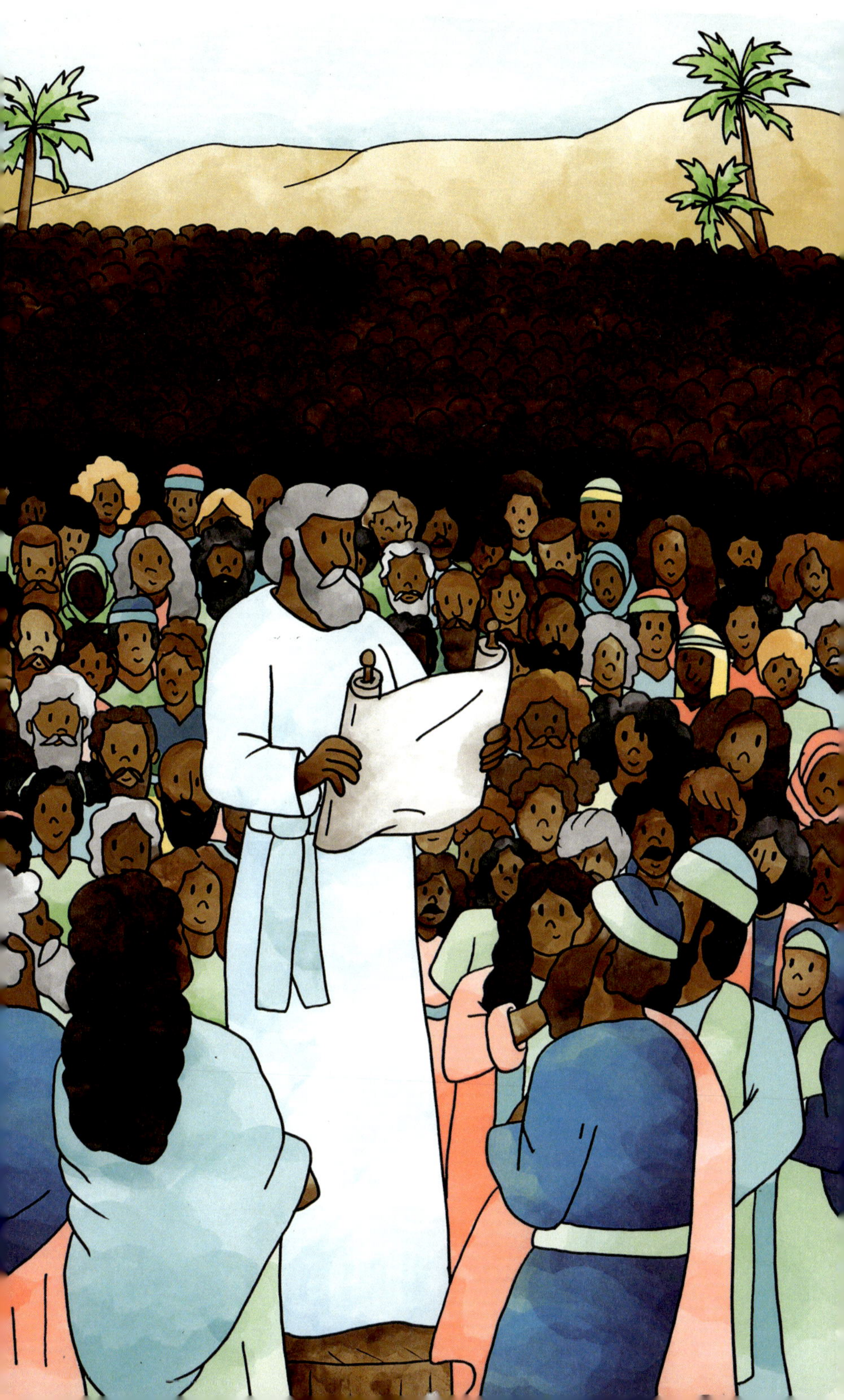

Kaleidoscope Corner
Tabernacle

The tabernacle was where God told His people to worship Him. It was like a very, very big tent where the Israelites came together to sing songs to God, offer sacrifices, receive forgiveness, and even hear from God...sort of like a church, but also very different in some ways. It was the center of life for Israel. That's why there are so many rules for the tabernacle—because it was God's tent.

Years later, John tells us that the new tabernacle is no longer a tent like the olden days. Now the tabernacle—the place where God lives with His people—is in His Son Jesus. We no longer have to go to a place to find God. God found us!

MORE COUNTING, MORE RULES, & A BENEDICTION

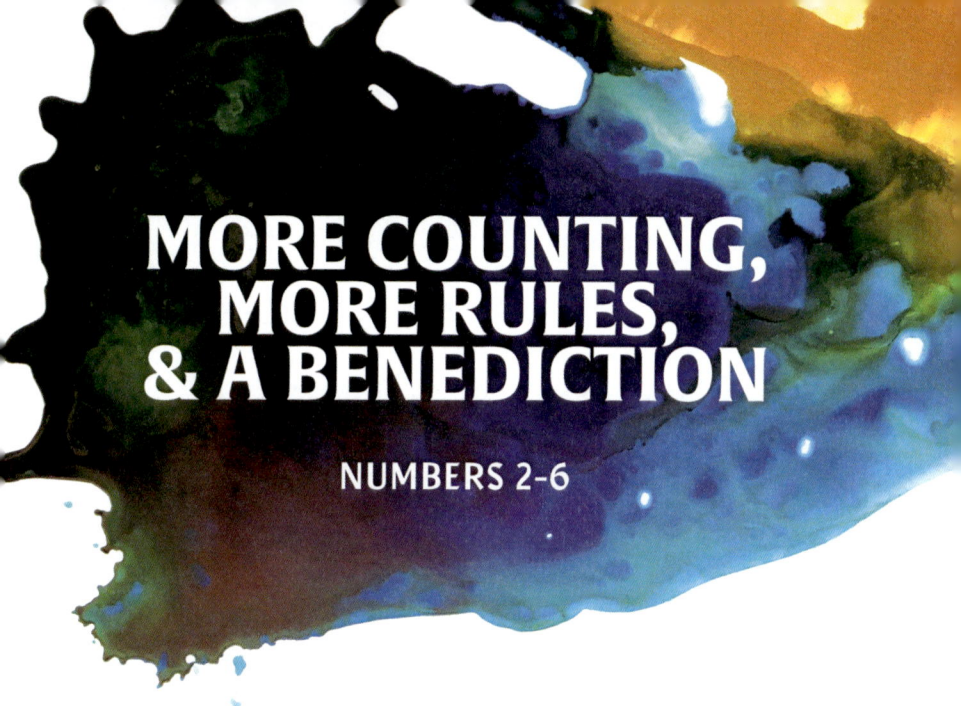

NUMBERS 2-6

Imagine you open your brand new board game and spill all the stuff inside out on the table. Then you count to make sure you have all the pieces you need to play the game. After that, you look at the instructions to set everything where it's supposed to go.

That's exactly what God did once Moses and his brother Aaron finished counting the people of Israel. God said, "Since there are so many people, we need to organize the camp. I'll tell you where everyone should pitch their tents and how they should march through the desert.

"First, on the east side, over where the sun rises in the morning, I want Judah, Zebulun, and Issachar to camp. They will be first in line when you march. Next, on the south side, tell Reuben, Simeon, and Gad to set up their camp. They will follow behind the first group.

"Right in the middle of the camp, you'll set up My tabernacle. Around the tabernacle will be the Levites, the special tribe I chose to care for and protect the tabernacle. They will be right in the middle of Israel to show everyone what the most important thing about Israel is—that you belong to the LORD and worship Me alone. The Levites will march carrying the tabernacle right in the middle of everyone.

"After that, on the west side will be Ephraim, Manasseh, and Benjamin. They will follow the tabernacle when they march. And last of all, on the north side, Dan, Asher, and Naphtali will camp. They will march at the very end."

Phew! Moses and Aaron likely needed a nice, long nap after all that!

Remember how God told Moses not to count the Levites earlier? Well, now He was ready to count them. Aaron's family was part of the tribe of Levi. They were going to be the priests—sort of like pastors—and be in charge of the rest of the Levites, with Aaron the high priest over them.

When they finished counting all 22,000 Levites, God explained, "Think back to the plagues in Egypt. Remember the last one? How could you forget it?! To punish Pharaoh for not letting my people go, I put to death every firstborn son in the land of Egypt. But, I had mercy and protected those who believed and obeyed me. I told you to sacrifice a lamb, put his blood on the doorframe of your houses, and I passed over your home. Your firstborn sons were spared!

"Well, the Levites are a reminder of My protection that night. Like the lamb that was sacrificed, the Levites will take the place of your firstborn sons—the ones I saved that day in Egypt. The ones who owed Me their lives."

After Moses counted the Levites, God divided up the tabernacle jobs and gave rules to protect Israel's bodies, souls, and marriages. Then He told them about a special promise they could make to God called the Nazirite vow.

Some men and women in Israel made this special Nazirite vow to God to take a break from normal life and spend time learning more about God's love for them and deepening their love for Him. After they made this promise, they'd follow a special set of rules: they couldn't eat or drink anything made from grapes or go to funerals or cut their hair. (If you know the story of Samson, this is what he was doing—well, what he was supposed to do, anyway!)

When the Nazirites decided to end this promised time with God, they went to the tabernacle, cut their long hair off, and burned it on the altar along with other sacrifices. Not everyone in Israel chose to do this, and it was not supposed to last forever. It was just a season of life set apart to spend extra time with God.

Last of all, God had one more wonderful command for Aaron and his family.

Why did God give all these rules? Why did God organize the Israelites this way? Why did God tell them to do all of these tabernacle jobs?

God did all this because of His immeasurable love for His people. Aaron and his sons, as the priests of Israel, were to remind God's people of this simple fact.

So, God's last wonderful command for Aaron and his family was to speak those good words of love to His people over and over.

"This is the blessing that you will say to My people," the LORD told Aaron and his sons. "This will remind them that they belong to Me and that I love them:

> "The Lord bless you and keep you.
> The Lord make His face to shine on you
> and be gracious to you.
> The Lord turn His face toward you
> and give you peace.

That is who I am: a God who blesses. And I want my people Israel to hold that truth in their hearts forever."

The Lord bless you and keep you the Lord make His face shine on you and be gracious to you the Lord turn His face toward you and give you peace.
Numbers 6:24-26

GOD'S BIG PARTY
NUMBERS 7-9

Put on your imagination glasses with me for a moment. You're at a birthday party. But this is no ordinary party because the fun doesn't stop for weeks!

Well, the Israelites didn't have to put on their imagination glasses, because God commanded them to do just that—to throw the biggest party ever!

Wait a second—usually when we think about God's commands, they don't sound very fun. This seemed different, though. God commanded His people to throw a huge, gigantic, unbelievable party that lasted for weeks! He wanted to celebrate His tabernacle because, in the tabernacle, He could be with the people He loved.

God told Moses, "Bring gifts to the tabernacle to consecrate it."

"Consecrate" means to gather to say, "This tabernacle is extraordinary and holy—it's not just any old regular place. It's special because God lives here."

So for twelve whole days, each of the twelve tribes took turns bringing gifts to the tabernacle to consecrate it. Each tribe brought a silver plate, a silver bowl, flour mixed with oil, a golden dish full of good-smelling incense, a bull, a ram, a baby boy lamb, a boy goat, two oxen, five more rams, five more boy goats, and five more baby boy lambs. That is one crazy, awesome party! And an animal house party at that!

But God reminded the people that the tabernacle deserved an epic party like this because when Moses went inside of it, he talked to God Himself!

Once the tabernacle was consecrated, God commanded Moses to consecrate the Levites, too. Remember, the Levites were the ones who would work at the tabernacle. All of the Levites took baths, cut their hair, washed their clothes, and made sure they were squeaky clean for their own party.

All the people went to the tabernacle, put their hands on the Levites, prayed for them, and offered sacrifices. Then God said, "Now the Levites belong to Me. Like I told you before, they will take the place of your firstborn sons—the ones who owe Me their lives for rescuing them from death in the land of Egypt. They will take care of My tabernacle and help the people of Israel pray and offer sacrifices for their sins."

After all this, the Levites were ready to serve. But God wasn't done partying quite yet.

He wanted Israel to celebrate again!

We've already heard God talk about the Passover a couple of times so far. The Passover was a remembrance of the night down in Egypt when the people sacrificed spotless lambs, put their blood on their doorframes, and God rescued all of the firstborn sons whose houses were marked with the lamb's blood. This was the final act of God that freed His people from slavery.

Without the Passover, there would be no Israel. No tabernacle. No parties. They would still be trapped in slavery. And God never wanted His people to forget this fantastic good news. No wonder He wanted them to celebrate!

So, God told them to reenact their last night in Egypt—put their shoes on like they were ready to escape and tell the story of God's rescue, all while eating a big feast of tasty lamb.

At last, came the grand finale. When the tabernacle was all set up, dark clouds rolled in and covered the tabernacle. At night, this same cloud burned like fire, lighting up the sky.

This was a theophany (to show that God was with the Israelites…see more about theophanies in the Kaleidoscope Corner at the end of the chapter). This cloud also let the Israelites know when it was time to set out and march. When the cloud moved, they followed it. As soon as the cloud stopped, they would set up their camp—every tribe going to the place where God commanded them.

Sometimes the cloud picked a place to stay for one or two days. Sometimes a month. Sometimes even longer than that. The Israelites never quite knew exactly how long they would be in a place. But they trusted God and followed Him wherever He told them to go through the desert.

Kaleidoscope Corner
Theophany
(*the-ah-fanny*)

There are a lot of funny-sounding words that Christians use, and this is one of them. But what does it mean? A theophany is a way that God appears to His people so they can see Him.

When God spoke to Moses as a burning bush? Theophany.

This cloud that appeared over the tabernacle and led Israel through the desert? Theophany.

God appeared to His people in thunder and lightning, earthquakes, and at times a mysterious figure called "the angel of the Lord." There's even a theophany in the New Testament in the book of Acts when the Holy Spirit came down on the disciples as a mighty wind and tongues of fire.

But Jesus—well, Jesus is not a theophany. He's not simply like God. Or a picture of God. He's the real thing. Jesus is really and truly God in a human body. 100% God, 100% human. Jesus shows us exactly who God is!

THE TROUBLE BEGINS

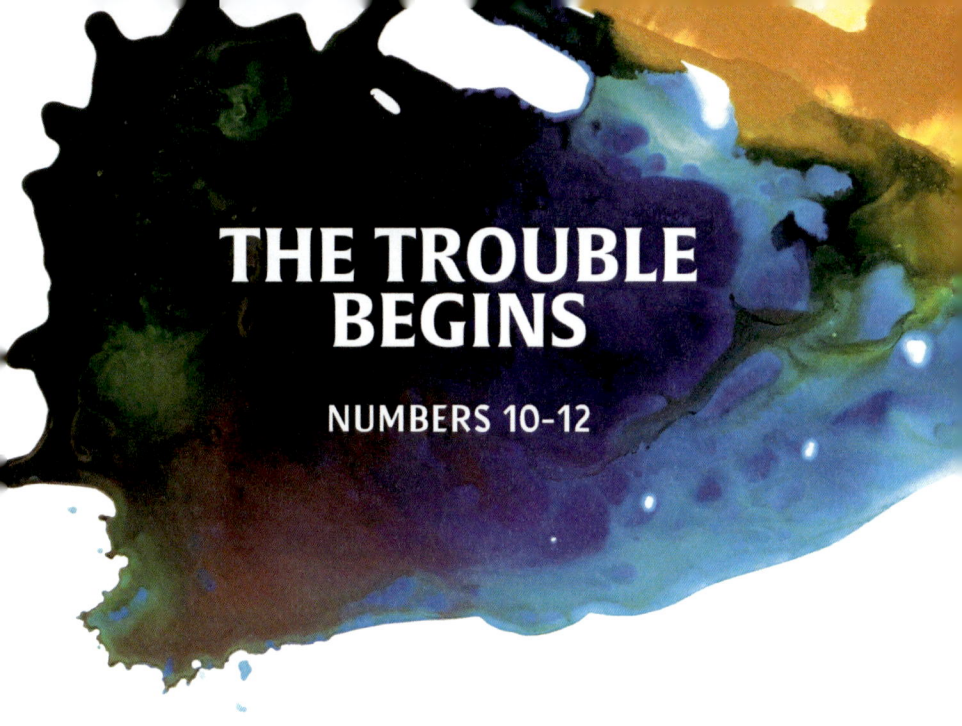

NUMBERS 10-12

A month later, out of the clear blue sky (pun intended!), the cloud over the tabernacle lifted and floated deeper into the desert like a huge balloon sailing away on a windy day. The leaders blew silver trumpets, letting everyone know that the day had come! It was time to leave.

Now, back in those days, there were no cars. But some people might have had donkeys—maybe even a camel or a wagon pulled by oxen. But even if they did have animals, they would have been loaded up with the people's stuff.

So the Israelites had to walk on foot. Imagine walking mile after mile after mile with hot desert sand crammed between your toes and no place to get relief from the scorching sun. You just might grumble and complain, stomp your feet, then grumble and complain some more!

And that's exactly what the Israelites did.

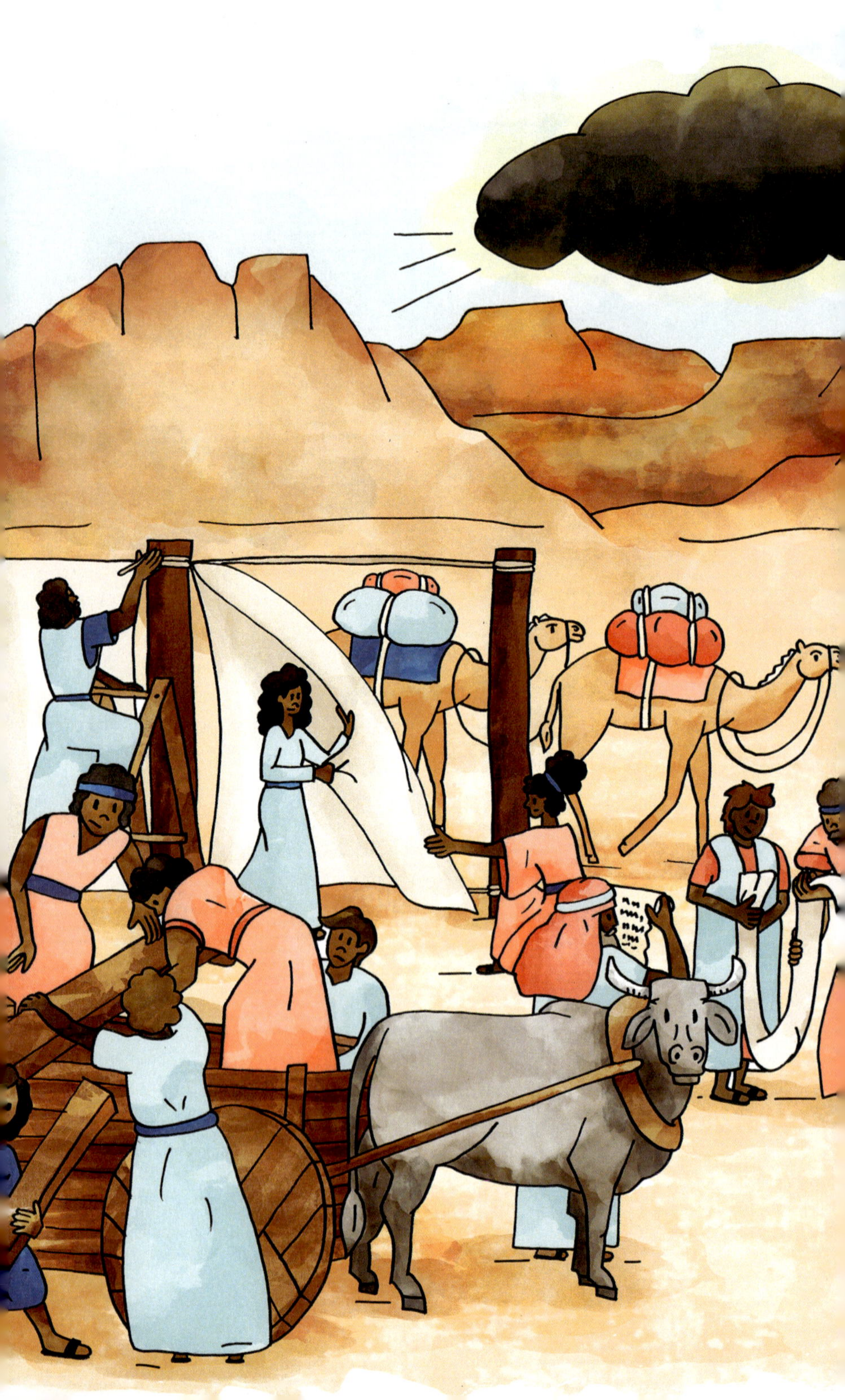

God grew angry at this grumbling—and that makes sense! Think of all the good things He'd done for Israel—saving them from Egypt, rescuing their firstborn, parting the Red Sea, giving them a tabernacle where they could talk with Him, and feeding them manna!

Oh yeah, the manna. Do you remember manna from earlier in the Bible? In the desert, there weren't any plants to eat or grocery stores to shop in. But God took care of Israel by feeding them manna—bread literally came down from heaven (it really did fall from the sky like snow)!

Well, manna wasn't exactly bread. It was little flakes that the people would gather from the ground every morning, crunch up, bake, and turn into bread. The bread was delicious, like cake—without the icing! What a miracle!

After eating manna every single day for more than a whole year, though, the people lost their taste for it. They even said, "We ate so much better back in Egypt! Think of all the different foods we had—fish and cucumbers and onions. Mmmm. Our slave masters provided for us better than God does! We want to go back to Pharaoh!" Can you believe that? No wonder God was mad!

All the complaining not only made God angry, but it also upset Moses. He cried out, "God, why did You bring me out here to take care of all these mumbly, grumbly people? I can't take this anymore!"

God agreed with Moses. "You're right. You need help. Find 70 leaders to help you, and I will fill them with My Spirit so they can guide the people with you. And as for these mumbly, grumbly people—if they're tired of the manna, I will give them some meat to eat.

"But not only one day, or two days, or five days, or ten days, or twenty days, but a whole month! "They'll have to eat meat until it comes out of their noses! They won't be able to even look at meat after this!"

Just as God said, the 70 leaders were filled with His Spirit and began sharing God's words with the people. Later on, a strong wind blew into the desert, and with the wind came birds called quail.

Not only a few quail, though, but piles and piles of quail. So many that you couldn't even walk without stepping on them!

The people were thrilled to finally have meat! They started snatching up all the birds and cooking them.

But they were gobbling up the quail so fast, they didn't even stop to thank God for sending it—or think about how they should thank Him for giving them manna day in and day out. In fact, they didn't thank God once for any of His other gifts of love to them at all!

While the meat was still stuck between their teeth, God grew angry with their mumbly, grumbly, and ungrateful hearts again and sent a plague into the Israelite camp.

Yep, a plague.

Just like the ones He sent on Pharaoh and the Egyptians. The greedy people with bellies full of quail died.

Now, you would think the people would learn their lesson about grumbling against God. But guess again...

It wasn't long before even Aaron and Miriam (Moses's sister) began grumbling, too. They were mad that Moses had married a Cushite woman because the land of Cush was a huge, powerful kingdom in Africa. To them, Moses seemed snooty and stuck-up because he married someone from a fancy place like that. The rest of the Israelites were simply a bunch of former slaves—not nearly as impressive as Cush. "Moses thinks he's better than us! God can speak to us too, you know!" Miriam and Aaron said.

But all that wasn't true. According to God, Moses was the most humble man in the world. So, like a father disciplining his arguing children, God said, "You three! Come here...right now!" The siblings scurried to the tabernacle and that great, dark cloud followed them.

In the cloud God said to Aaron and Miriam, "I speak to a lot of people, you're right. But when I do, it's in dreams or visions. But not with My faithful servant Moses. I speak to Moses face to face. You have no right to talk about My friend Moses that way!"

Then as quickly as the cloud entered the tabernacle, it left. And when Moses, Aaron, and Miriam looked around at one another, they realized that Miriam's skin had turned as white as snow and was all shriveled up!

Right away, Moses dropped to his knees and prayed, "God, forgive my sister! Heal her, please!"

God replied, "She will get better. But until then, she needs to stay outside the camp of Israel. After seven days, she can come back."

Sure enough, after seven days, Miriam was healed, came back to Israel's camp, and God's people marched out again—deeper into the desert.

Kaleidoscope Corner
God's Anger

Was it strange to see God's anger in this chapter? We don't usually think of God as angry, right? We think of Him as loving, kind, and caring.

Those things are true, of course. But God gets angry too. What makes Him angry is actually the very thing that makes Him loving! The Bible shows us that sin makes God angry because our sin can hurt us, it can hurt others, and it even hurts God's heart as well. God knows that obeying His commands is the only way that we can enjoy life the way He wants us to.

Now, is God's anger only something that we see in the Old Testament before Jesus comes to earth? Not at all! Jesus gets angry too.

In the Gospel of John, for example, Jesus storms into the temple (like the tabernacle in Numbers) where people were trying to worship God, but a group of merchants was more interested in selling them stuff. Jesus grew angry because He wanted His house to be a place of worship. Jesus' anger in the temple, just like in the rest of the Bible, shows God's love for us.

We'll see a lot of God's anger in Numbers, but even more than that, we will see His forgiveness. God's forgiveness is deeper than any sea and higher than any cloud because of what Jesus did for His people. God's own Son would one day die on a cross, absorbing all the anger God has toward our sin. Because of Jesus, all that is left in God's heart for His people is love.

A HAPPY DAY TURNED SAD

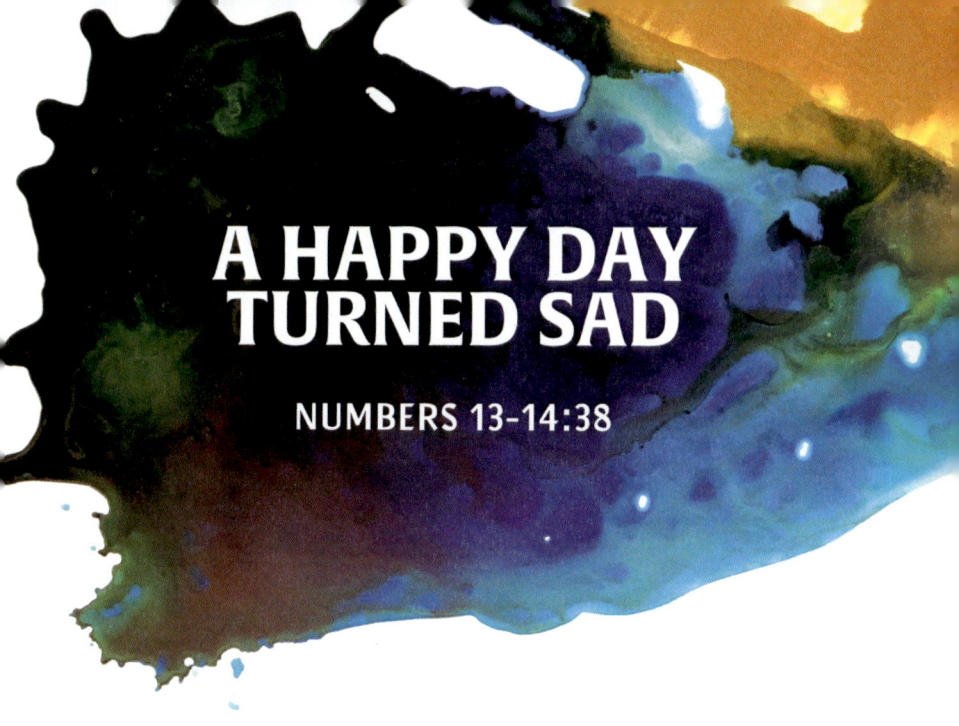

NUMBERS 13-14:38

Imagine squinting your eyes as the bright desert sun screams through the clouds. You can barely make out several hazy figures walking in the distance. "They're back! They're back!" you hear someone shout far away.

"They are back! The spies are back!" you think. *"With news of the Promised Land!"*

Forty days earlier, God told Moses, "Send men to spy out the land of Canaan—the Promised Land that I'm giving to Israel."

So, Moses picked twelve men, one from each of the twelve tribes, and gave them orders. "Go into the hills of Canaan and take notes on what it's like up there. Are there a lot of people or just a few? Are they strong or weak? Is the land green and lush or sandy and desert-y? Do they have big houses or tents like us? Be brave!"

Now, they were finally here! As a bonus, they brought souvenirs—fruits that looked juicy and tasty. They even had a bunch of grapes so big that it had to be carried by two men on a thick pole!

The spies were exhausted, but also eager to tell the people all about Canaan. "The land was beautiful—as if it were flowing with milk and honey. I mean, feast your eyes on this fruit we brought! That's the good news. But there's bad news, too.

"The bad news is that there is no way we can beat the people in battle—they would wipe the floor with us!"

But Caleb, one of the twelve who went to spy out the land disagreed. "Hold on just a second! We could go up there right now and defeat them—we have God on our side!"

"No way," ten of the other spies said. "The people up there are strong. And not only do they live in houses and not tents, but the houses are built like fortresses. We're not lying to you when we say that the people of Canaan are actual giants.

"We think they must be the great-great-great-grandchildren of the giants of old! Standing next to them, we looked like tiny grasshoppers! So, we shouldn't go back up there, unless we want to get squashed like bugs."

As the people listened, they grew worried. Some even wept all night. The next day, though, people weren't crying anymore. They were grumbling about Moses and Aaron again.

"I wish we had died back in Egypt!"

"Even dying in this awful desert would be better than dying in battle against giants!"

"Why did God drag us all out here just to die?"

"Don't you think it would be better if we just pack up and head back to Egypt?"

"It sure would! Let's pick a different leader than Moses or Aaron and go back there right this minute!"

When Moses and Aaron heard the people say such ridiculous things, they dropped to their faces and prayed for God to forgive the Israelites. Caleb and Joshua, the only two of the twelve spies that believed God, tore their clothes and shouted at the people, "No! What are you thinking? God loves us! This is the land He gave us! He will give us victory in the battle! The Canaanites don't stand a chance! God is with us. Don't be afraid of them."

But the people were so afraid of fighting the Canaanites that they began gathering stones to kill Caleb, Joshua, Moses, and Aaron! But right before they could, that cloud of God's presence went back inside the tabernacle.

"How long will my own people hate Me, Moses?" God asked. "How long will they refuse to believe in Me even though I keep performing miracles and providing for them? Maybe I should start all over again—as I did with Noah and the flood."

But Moses replied, "Don't do it, LORD. These are Your people. Even though they deserve it, if You start over, the other nations will think You are not powerful enough to bring them into the Promised Land and keep Your promises. Remember what kind of God You told me You are? A God who is slow to anger. A God whose love never ends. A God who forgives people even though they don't deserve it. A God who, like a good father, makes rules to love and protect His children. Please forgive the great sin of Your people because of Your never-ending love. Forgive them like You have forgiven them over and over again during this whole journey in the desert all the way from Egypt."

God responded, "As you asked, I have forgiven them. But as surely as I live and as surely as My glory will fill the whole earth, none of the people who came out of Egypt—these people who have tested my patience and goodness time and time again, even though they saw My amazing miracles—not a single one of them will journey into the Promised Land.

"All those people you counted—those who are 20 years old and older who keep on grumbling against Me—will live the rest of their lives wandering in the desert. The only ones who get to enter the Promised Land are Caleb and Joshua. They are faithful to Me and trust in My power. Tomorrow, we will turn around and head back deeper into the desert... away from Canaan."

What a sad day for the people of Israel! They broke the heart of their God who saved them! And now, the goal of getting to the Promised Land seemed impossible.

Kaleidoscope Corner
Praying God's Character & Promises

If you read closely, you'll see two main ways that Moses prays: God's promises and God's character. These are ways that we can pray to God now as well!

We know that God makes a lot of promises in the Bible. For the Israelites, He promised that He would save them from slavery, protect them, bring them into the Promised Land, and more.

Moses reminded God of these promises. Now, of course, God never actually forgets anything. Reminding God of these promises is simply asking God to do what He has already said He will do. It also helps us remember and believe His promises.

Moses also prayed about God's character. Character is what a person is like deep, down inside.

How did Moses know God's character?

God talked to Moses when He was on the mountain getting the Ten Commandments.

God told Moses the exact words that Moses repeats in his prayer. "A God who takes a long time to get angry. A God whose love never ends. A God who forgives people even though they don't deserve it. A God who makes good rules and expects people to follow them." Moses was asking God to show everyone just how loving and forgiving He was in the way He treated Israel, even though they sinned.

Try it out. When you pray today, remember some promises God has made to His people. Remember some of the best things you love about God. Then, talk to God about those things!

CONSEQUENCES & COMMITMENT

NUMBERS 14:39-15:21

Moses delivered the sad news to the people. Not a single person older than 20 years old would be able to enter the Promised Land, except for Joshua and Caleb. Even though they saw all of God's miracles—the plagues in Egypt, the Red Sea opening up for them to walk through on dry land, manna from heaven, and on and on—God's people still didn't believe God would take care of them.

When they heard this, the people cried their eyes out. Now it was certain; they would never get what they longed for.

So, the people began hatching a plan to fix everything all by themselves.

"We don't want to be stuck in this desert forever!"

"Did you see how juicy and delicious all that fruit from Canaan was?"

"I sure did! Didn't Caleb say that we could defeat those Canaanites in battle? Let's make a plan to go up there first thing in the morning."

Early the next day, the people crowded around Moses. "We're here, Moses. We were wrong. We sinned against God. But now we have a plan to go to Canaan and fight just like God told us."

"No way! Don't do it," Moses said. "God won't go with you. You'll be alone, and you know you can't defeat the Canaanites without Him! God's punishment is final!"

Do you think the people listened to Moses? Of course not! They're really bad at that. They simply shrugged their shoulders, grabbed their weapons, and marched up to the hills of Canaan—all by themselves, without God's protection.

Close your eyes, picture it—what do you think happened? I'd imagine you can make a good guess.

As soon as they got close to Canaan, the enemies picked up their swords and hurried out to fight the Israelites. Soon the Israelites knew they were losing, dropped their weapons, and scurried back home like little mice with a hungry cat right on their tails.

God had made His decision to keep Israel from the Promised Land, and God's decision was final.

So is that it? Is this the end of the story? Will God stop being friends with His people? The Israelites didn't trust God and disobeyed Him over and over. They tried to enter the Promised Land on their own without His help...and it was clear that God was not changing His mind. But God couldn't stop loving His people. He simply would not give up on His promises!

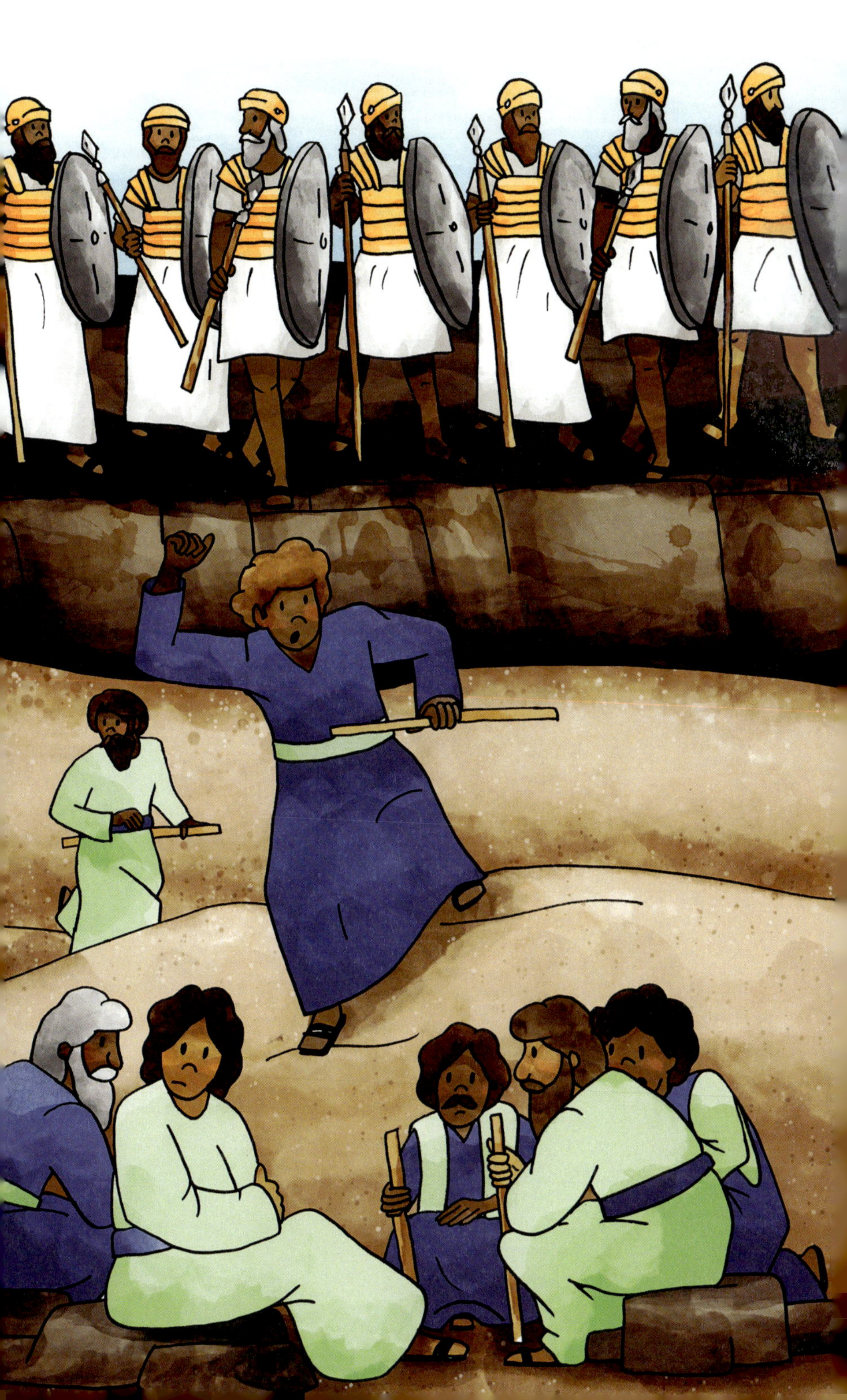

"Moses," the LORD said. "Go and tell Israel this: one day, a long time from now, you will live in the Promised Land once again. As I've already told you, it will take forty years. I won't change my mind about that. And when you finally get to the Promised Land, it won't be because you are so smart and brave. No! I will give it to you as a gift.

"You can't rebuild what you tore down on your own. You're not strong enough. Only I am strong enough. I will rebuild our friendship.

"You deserve to be punished for what you did, but because I am merciful, an animal will sacrifice its life and will be punished for you. Even though you should die, the sacrifice will die instead."

Then God rolled out a long list of rules for the sacrifices. But the sacrifices were not only for Israel. You see, God's plan is more wonderful than that. His good news is for everyone who would trust Him. The sacrifices were also for people from other nations who loved the Lord. These "outsiders" could make the same sacrifices as Israel and be welcomed into the family of God.

Though the Israelites had turned their back on God and been punished, He gave them the gift of forgiveness and was opening His arms even wider to welcome more people into friendship with Him.

But this gift of an animal sacrifice was only a whisper of what was to come. One day, many years later, God would send Jesus as the ultimate sacrifice. But Jesus's death wouldn't welcome us into the Promised Land. No, the gift of Jesus is much more magnificent than that. It welcomes us into our eternal home—a place where sickness, sadness, and death are no more.

Kaleidoscope Corner
Forgiveness from God

Like the Israelites, we all sin against God. We want to do things our way instead of His. We disobey the parents He gave us. We are unloving toward our brothers and sisters and friends.

So how do we put things back together with God after we tear them all up with our sin?

Pretend you have a dirty mirror. You want to clean it, but all you have are filthy rags. What happens when you take one of your rags and rub it on a dirty mirror? Does it clean the mirror? Or does it make it worse?

Sometimes we try to trick God into loving us again. We think, "If I do a lot of good stuff, maybe God will forget about all the bad stuff I did." But the Bible tells us that this is like rubbing filthy rags on an already dirty mirror—it doesn't make things better. It actually makes them worse.

That's what the Israelites did when they fought Canaan without God's help. Instead, God gave them sacrifices to heal their relationship with Him—something else taking the punishment they deserved for disobeying.

Today, we have an even better sacrifice. Jesus died on the cross. He didn't sin at all. But we, who sin a lot, stand forgiven because Jesus took the punishment that we should get. If we believe that Jesus is strong enough to save and forgive us, He certainly will.

HEY, WHO'S IN CHARGE?

NUMBERS 16-17:11

Israel's trust in God was, well, wobbly at best. They didn't think He was powerful enough to bring them into the Promised Land. So, God punished His people.

Would anyone in Israel trust and obey God?

Remember God's special tribe, the Levites? They were supposed to take care of the tabernacle. Certainly, if anyone listened to God, the Levites would…right?!

One day a man from the tribe of Levi, named Korah, gathered the leaders of the people. Together they stormed up to Moses and Aaron, demanding, "Every single Israelite can speak with God. We don't need you to boss us around! And besides, who put the two of you in charge anyway?! You don't seem to be doing a very good job!"

Moses heard them, but he didn't fight back or get angry. Instead, he fell on his face in prayer, saying, "In the morning, the LORD will show you His special leader. Do this: take a fire pot and burn it before the LORD tomorrow, and God will choose His holy one. It is not Aaron and me who have gone too far! You have gone too far, sons of Levi!"

Then Moses reminded Korah, "Do you think it was a small thing for God to choose your tribe out of all the others to serve Him in His tabernacle and to care for His people? That's not enough? You want to be the leaders, too? You aren't grumbling against Moses and Aaron. Instead, you are grumbling against God Himself!"

The next day, Korah and his friends took their fire pots, as did Aaron. They lit fires inside the pots and placed them in front of the tabernacle with Moses and Aaron. Then, that great cloud of God's presence appeared before everyone who was watching. And God told Moses and Aaron, "Tell all the people to step away from Korah and his friends."

Moses shouted to everyone, "The LORD made me the leader of Israel—none of this was my idea! If nothing happens to Korah and his friends, you'll know that I am lying. But if something new happens, something no one has ever seen before, then you will know that these men have disobeyed the LORD."

And as soon as Moses finished saying these words, the ground underneath Korah and his friends cracked open. Korah, all of his stuff, and all of his friends fell into the crack, just as if the earth had swallowed them whole! Then, as quickly as the ground opened up, it closed back shut. Everyone stood in shock, looked around with pancake-sized eyes, then ran for their lives!

"The earth is going to swallow us up, too!"

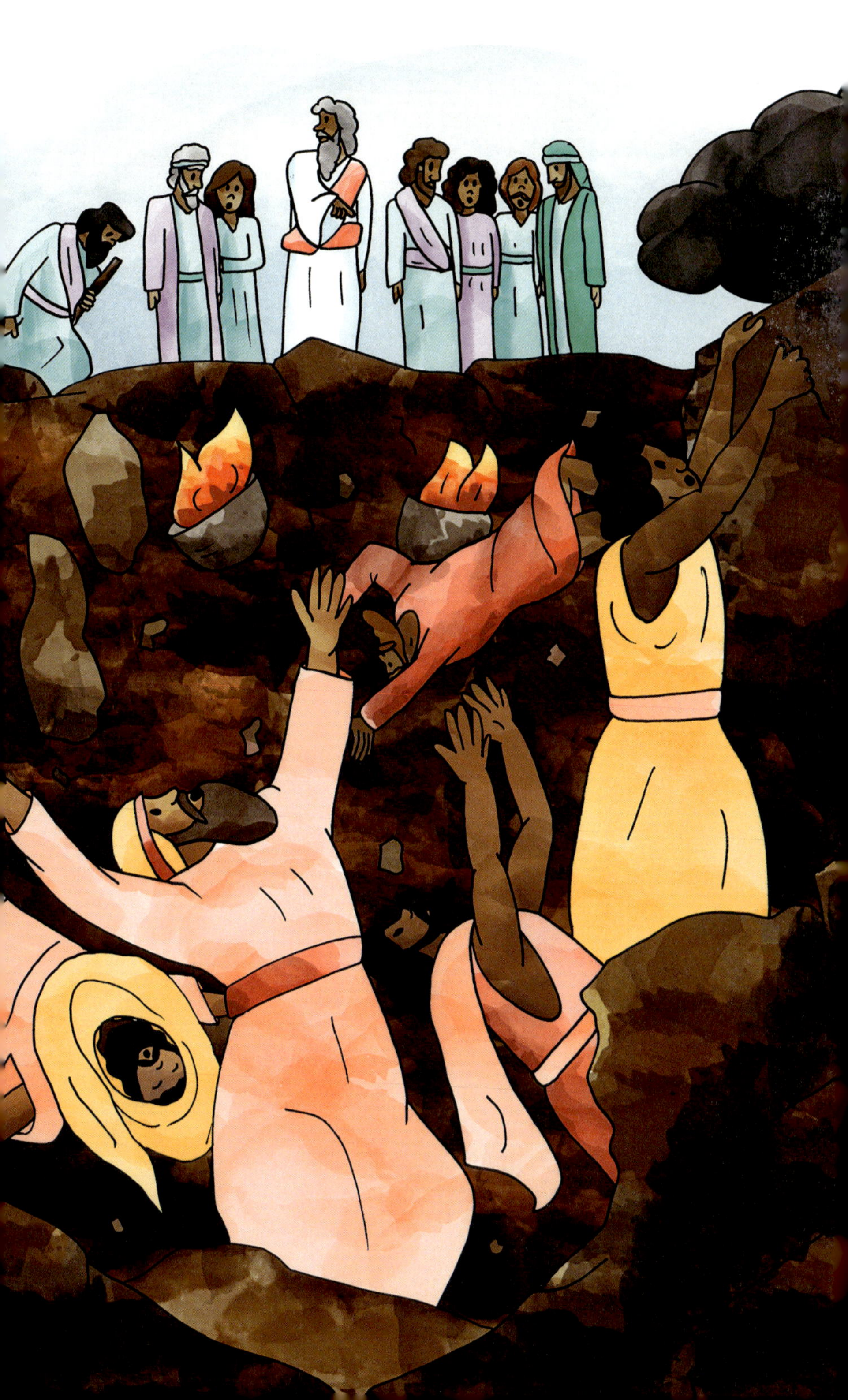

It wasn't too long before the Israelites blamed Moses and Aaron for everything that happened with Korah and his friends! They still didn't believe that God was the one who put Moses and Aaron in charge.

So the LORD told Moses, "Go get the staffs (kind of like walking sticks) of the leaders of the tribes—twelve staffs total. Write their names on each of the staffs. For the staff of Levi, write Aaron's name. Then place all twelve of them in the middle of the tabernacle. Whichever staff comes alive and sprouts leaves and flowers is the staff of my chosen man. Maybe this will help the Israelites with their grumbling problem!"

The next day, when Moses went back inside the tabernacle, Aaron's staff was covered in leaves and flowers, and even almonds! Moses took the staffs outside to show the people what happened. Each man took his staff, but God told Moses, "Put Aaron's staff back inside the tabernacle as a reminder for all these grumbly people. Let them never forget who's in charge." Moses did exactly as God said.

Kaleidoscope Corner
Miracles

The first several books of the Bible, including the book of Numbers, are full of miracles. You also see some later during the lives of Elijah and Elisha. Then in the New Testament, in the time of Jesus and the apostles, we see lots of miracles again. We don't usually see miracles in our lives, right?

But, if you think about it another way, everything that happens during the day is a miracle. Every time our heart beats. Every breath in our lungs. The sun rising in the morning and setting in the evening. The stars shining brightly in the sky.

But sometimes God does something outside of what He normally does to show His power, like the miracles we just read about in Numbers— opening the earth up and making a dead stick grow flowers.

Other times, His miracles show us what the world is supposed to be like. When Jesus was on earth, one of the things He loved to do was heal sick people. He did this to show His power, but also to remind us that God doesn't like it when we are sick. It simply wasn't how He made the world to work best.

And with these miracles, Jesus also reminds us that because He rose from the dead, we can know that one day we will be with Him forever where there will be no sickness or pain or crying or death.

FAILING THE TEST

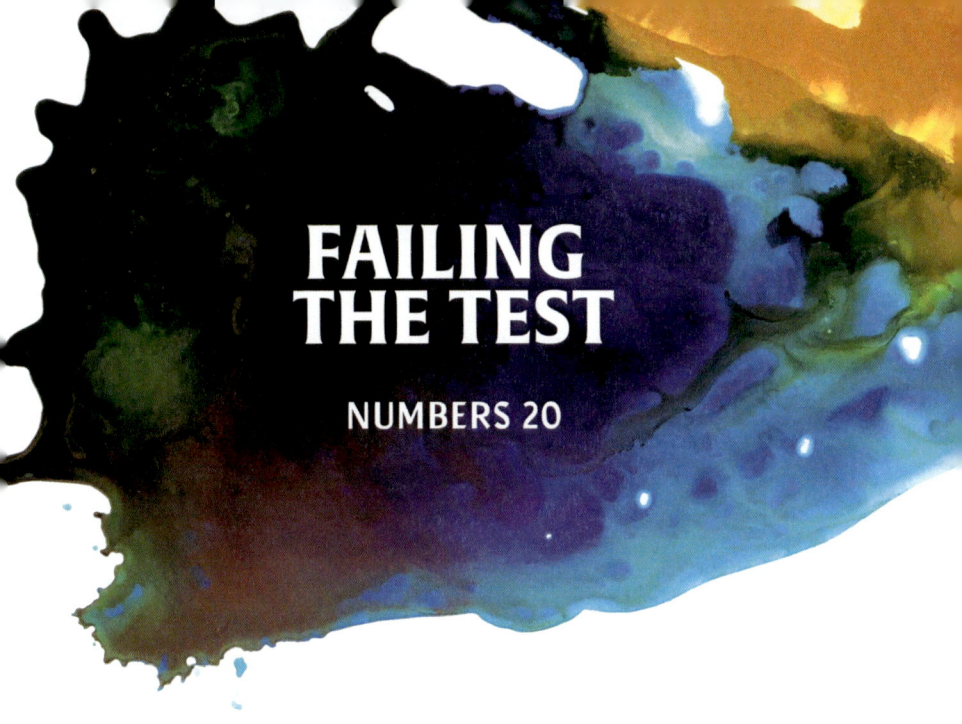

NUMBERS 20

Week after week, mile after mile, the people walked and crawled and trudged through the hot desert. As they journeyed, those who didn't trust God grew old and died. When the Israelites arrived at a place called Kadesh, someone important drew her last breath—Miriam, Moses's big sister.

She was the one who followed Moses down the river in the basket when he was a baby—the one who helped save his life. The disobedient Israelites buried her and so many others who died along the way, out in the dry desert, far away from the land God promised them.

"I wish we had all been swallowed up by the earth that day with Korah and his people!"

"Moses and Aaron, why in the world did you bring us all out into the wilderness?"

"Do you just want us and all our animals to die?"

"Yeah! Why did you take us away from our home in Egypt to this evil place?"

"There's no food—no grain or figs or vines or fruit! There's not even any water to drink!"

Like they had done so many times before, Moses and Aaron ran to the tabernacle and fell on their faces in prayer to hear what the LORD wanted to tell them.

Then, the cloud of God's presence came, saying, "Take the staff and gather the people, you and Aaron, and while they watch, tell the rock to give them water. Then, water will flow from the rock like never before. It will be a miracle so great, it could only be done by God."

This all sounded quite odd, but Moses trusted God. So, he grabbed the staff and went to do just what the LORD commanded.

Moses shouted to the people gathered at the rock, "Listen up, all you rebels! You want water? We'll give you water! From this rock!"

Moses grabbed the staff, raised it over his head, and slammed it onto the rock, not once, but two times.

But wait, didn't God tell Moses to speak to the rock? Why was Moses beating the rock with his staff?!

Even though water poured out for the people and their animals as God said, Moses had disobeyed the LORD.

Then God spoke again to Moses and Aaron: "Because you did not believe Me, and because you did not honor Me in front of the people by obeying Me, neither of you will lead the people into the land that I have given them."

These waters were named Meribah, which means "arguing," because the people argued with the LORD there.

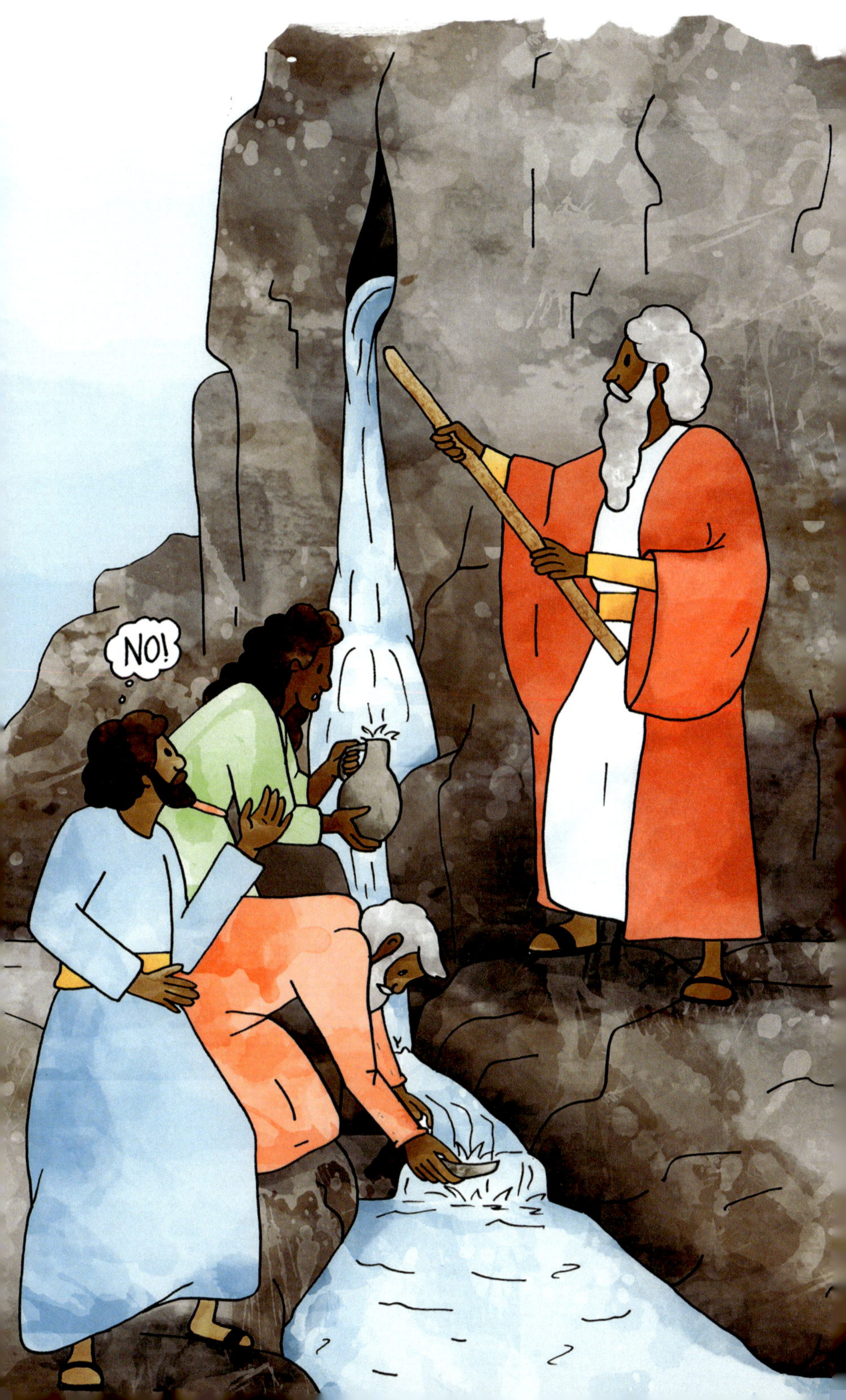
NO!

The Israelites did not think God was strong or good enough to keep His promise and bring them safely into the land that the spies saw. The Levites, the special tribe of Israel, did not trust the leaders God had chosen and wanted to be in charge themselves.

And Moses—who spoke with God face to face and prayed for the Israelites to be forgiven when they sinned—even Moses lost his temper and did things his way instead of doing as God asked. In the desert, all of the people turned away from God. They were tempted and sinned. They did not trust the LORD who loved them.

They all failed the test.

The Israelites journeyed on and soon came to a mountain. The cloud stopped moving, and the people started setting up their camp like always.

Then God said to Moses and Aaron, "Aaron, because you disobeyed and turned your back on me at Meribah, you will not enter the Promised Land with the people. Moses, take Aaron and his son Eleazar up to the top of this mountain. When you get there, take off Aaron's priestly robes and put them on his son Eleazar. And Aaron will be brought to his parents and grandparents and great grandparents—he will die there."

What a sad moment for Israel!

Moses did what God asked. He led old Aaron and his son Eleazar up the mountain, took Aaron's robes off, and placed them on Eleazar, the new high priest.

As Moses and Eleazar came walking down the mountain, the people knew that Aaron had died. For days and days on end, the people of God wailed and cried at the loss of their beloved friend.

Kaleidoscope Corner
Temptation

Do you know that feeling when you think about doing something you know you are not supposed to? Maybe there are some cookies in the kitchen that your parents told you are for something special, but every time you walk by, you smell their tasty goodness. It's like there are two of you—one who wants to do the right thing and obey your parents, and the other who wants to do the wrong thing and gobble up a delicious cookie.

That feeling is called temptation in the Bible. Temptation is not sin. It comes before sin. It's when your own mind or someone else tells you, "It's ok. No one will know. Just take one cookie. They won't even know it's gone!" When you feel or hear this, you can say "No" or you can say "Yes."

In the Garden of Eden, the serpent tempted Adam and Eve, saying, "God said you couldn't eat that fruit, but He didn't really mean it. Look how beautiful it is!" Adam and Eve were tempted, and then they sinned.

Numbers shows us that no matter what, even if we're in the middle of a dry desert, we should always trust God's words over every other voice. We should always remember that God is the one who cares for us.

Did you know that even Jesus was tempted? The Bible says He was tempted just as we are. But, Jesus never said "Yes" to temptation. He only obeyed His Father all the time. In fact, He obeyed for us! So that He could be the perfect Savior of the world.

HINTS OF HOPE
NUMBERS 21

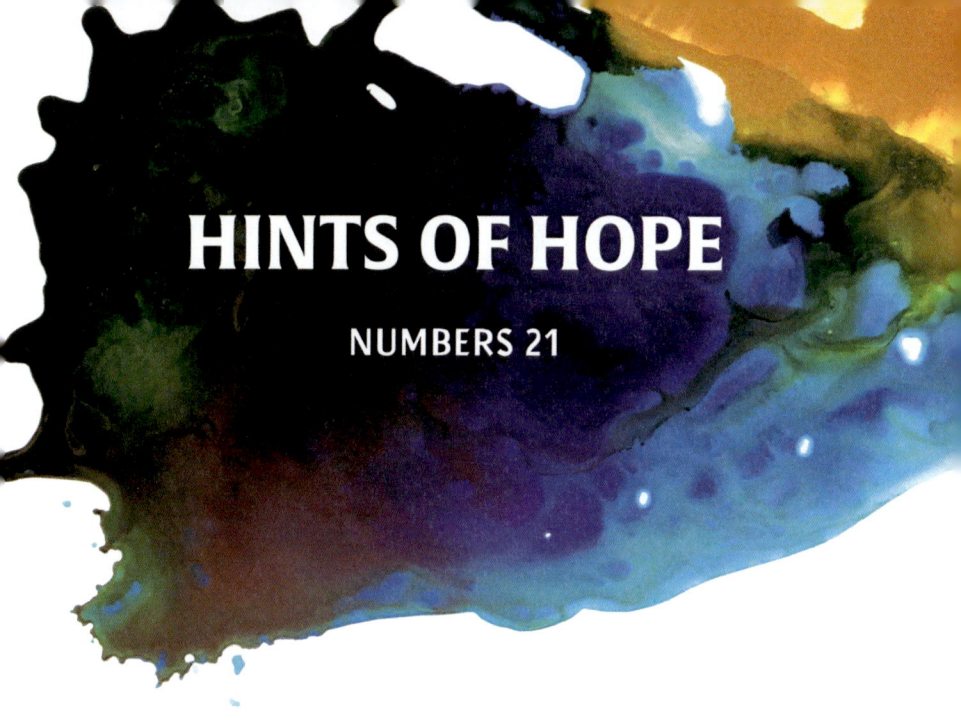

Everything sure felt hopeless for Israel. God's people complained every day. Nearly all of the spies feared the Canaanites more than they trusted God.

The Levites wanted to be in charge.

Miriam and Aaron were dead.

Even Moses himself was no longer allowed to lead the people into the Promised Land.

It felt like the last puny candle in a big, dark room was about to burn out. But, in the middle of all that darkness and sadness, the Israelites began to see hints of hope.

One day, while the Israelites were dragging their hot, sandy feet through the desert, they started to lose their patience.

"Why?! Why?! Why did you take us out of Egypt only to die in the middle of nowhere?!"

"There's no food and no water anywhere and the little bit of food we do have is nasty! Yuck!"

When God heard their grumbling, He made snakes appear out of nowhere! Can you imagine? Snakes! Everywhere! Slithering and squirming all around. And these weren't your friendly "pet shop variety." No, they were poisonous and began biting and sinking their long, sharp fangs into anyone they could get to!

All of a sudden, the people changed their tune. "Moses, Moses, Moses! We're *so* sorry for what we said about you and the LORD. Please pray to God so that He will take all these awful snakes away. Hurry!"

Moses did what they asked and prayed to God. But God didn't make the snakes go poof! and disappear. Instead, He told Moses to do something strange. God said, "Make a fiery serpent out of bronze and place it on a pole. If someone is bitten and looks at the pole, they will live." That's it! All they had to do was look at this metal snake up on a pole, and their snake-bitten skin would heal. How amazing! How easy!

Many years later, Jesus told His people that He was like this snake. When He was nailed to the cross and lifted up high, everyone would see Him like this metal snake in the wilderness. But Jesus wouldn't only save His people from snake bites. No, He would save them from something much worse—the sting of death.

Even in the middle of their complaining, God was saving His people and showing them a picture of how He would one day rescue them from the poison in their hearts—sin.

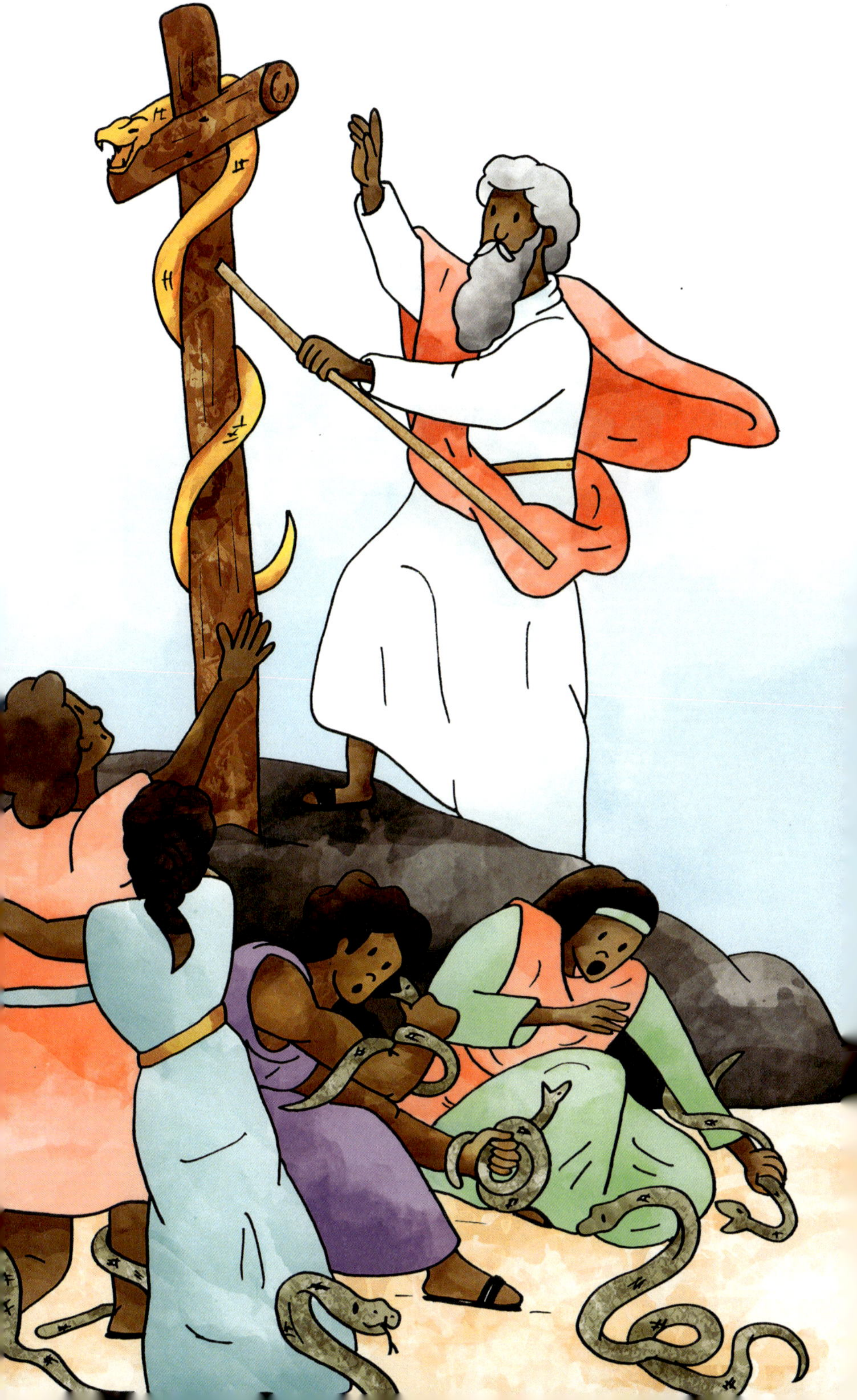

But the life-saving snake was not the only hopeful sign for Israel. One day, when they were traveling, they came across wells—full of water! Ice-cold, delicious, wonderful water! There's simply no way we can understand how happy they were to find this water in the middle of the desert. It was even tastier than a frozen fruity popsicle on a hot summer day!

As the water hit their sandpaper-dry mouths for the first time, they began to sing with excitement! These Israelites, who complained almost every time they opened their mouths, were now singing with joy at the taste of this refreshing water!

I bet you can imagine how strong the Israelites felt after drinking that delectable water! They were recharged and ready to continue their journey through the hot, sandy desert to reach the Promised Land.

So, Israel packed up their belongings and continued walking. But there was another problem—yes, another one!

You see, not everyone was pleased to meet Israel as they walked to the Promised Land. Some people were even downright mean!

Two of those mean people were evil kings named Sihon and Og. If I had names like that, I might be grumpy too!

The bad news for Israel is that they had to travel through the kingdoms of Sihon and Og to get where they were going.

So, they did what you or I might do and wrote a very polite letter.

> "Hello sirs, may we travel through your land? We promise not to eat or drink anything along the way—we have all that we need already. You won't even know we're there!"

But the kings didn't like the letter. Not only did Sihon and Og not want the Israelites to come anywhere near them, they even sent their armies to fight God's people, even though Israel didn't do anything to them!

But Sihon and Og were missing something that Israel had...God.

The same Israelites who were shaking in their boots just thinking about fighting the Canaanites were now chasing the armies of Sihon and Og as they ran away scared.

No doubt about it, God had given them victory in battle—and they knew He would give them victory again in the Promised Land. Maybe they could be hopeful after all!

A WIZARD & HIS TALKING DONKEY

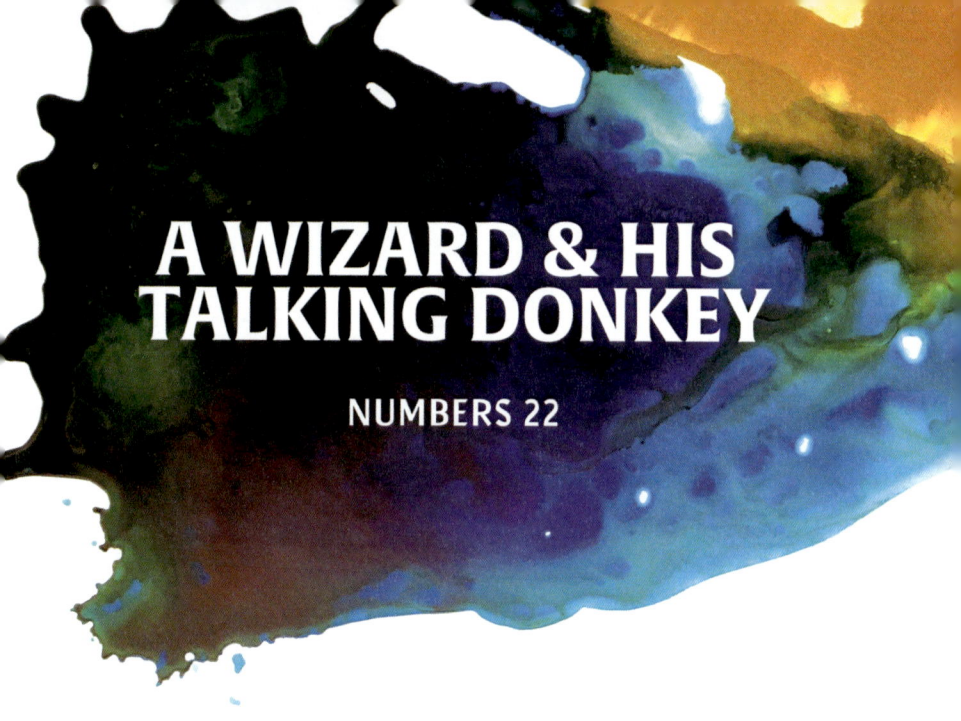

NUMBERS 22

So far in our story, the main characters have been our beloved, but bratty Israelites. We've seen their journey through the desert, their temptation, their sin, and God's love. But what about the other people, called Moabites, who lived nearby? What did they think about this strange group of people carrying a giant tent and following a cloud through the desert? Let's listen to this weird story and find out!

"Your Highness," the messenger said, panting like a dog on a hot day. "The Israelites—those people who came out of Egypt—the people that defeated Pharaoh and Sihon and Og—they just set up their camp—right down the road."

King Balak of Moab began to tremble. He'd heard stories about the Israelites and their powerful God. "Oh no. The Israelites will gobble us up like an ox munching grass."

The people of Moab were terrified. What could they do now?

Balak had an idea. Far away, there was a famous sorcerer (like a wizard) named Balaam. If Israel's God was what made them so powerful, maybe, just maybe, Balaam could trick their God into being on Balak's side so Moab could defeat Israel in battle.

Could this plan work? After all, Israel had been so mumbly, grumbly, and unloving to God for almost forty years in the desert. Maybe God was tired of them. Maybe God would join teams with Balak after all!

All the leaders of Moab set out to search for Balaam. They took lots of money with them to see if they could tempt this famous sorcerer to work for them.

When they arrived, Balaam thought and thought. "Hmmm...why don't you spend the night here. I'll see if Israel's God will talk to me. If He says it's ok, then I'll go with you."

That night, God actually did appear to Balaam! He warned the sorcerer, "Do not go with these leaders from Moab. Israel belongs to Me. I have blessed them, and I will never take My blessing away."

So Balaam got up the next morning and told the leaders, "Sorry, no can do. Their God won't let me."

The leaders went back to King Balak to break the bad news. But Balak wouldn't change his mind. "We have to get Balaam to help us! Go back with more leaders and take even more money with you this time!" The leaders did just that. They traveled hundreds of miles back to Balaam's house, then knocked on his door again. "Please, Balaam! Help us by putting a curse on the Israelites."

Again, Balaam told them the same thing. "Stay here for the night, and I'll see what their God says."

This time God said, "You can go with them, but only if you do and say exactly what I tell you." Balaam thought about all the money and smiled. The next morning, he saddled his donkey and left with the leaders of Moab.

But God grew angry with Balaam because He knew that all Balaam cared about was the loads of money he would get for helping Moab. God wanted to make sure Balaam remembered who was in charge and that Balaam would speak only God's words.

So God sent the angel of the LORD (another one of those theophanies we talked about earlier). But, curiously enough, only Balaam's donkey could see the angel standing in the road, holding a giant sword.

The donkey was immediately startled and ran right off the road. Balaam, not knowing what to make of his donkey's behavior, hit her in anger. He eventually led her back to the road, but the donkey saw the angel again, tried to bolt, and squished Balaam's foot up against a wall. Balaam was furious, and he hit her again.

Finally, Balaam hopped back on the donkey and started riding again. Once again, the donkey saw the angel right in front of her, so she stopped right in her tracks and sat down on the road.

Balaam was about to lose his mind! He hit his donkey as hard as he could with his staff. But before Balaam could strike his donkey one more time, God had something mind-blowing in store.

The donkey opened her mouth and begin talking, "Hey! Knock it off already! What did I ever do to you?!"

Balaam talked back to his donkey without even thinking about how bizarre this whole situation was! He must have been really mad! "You made me look like a clown! I wish I had a sword and not just my staff—I'd kill you right now!"

The donkey replied, "Haven't I always been a good donkey for you? You've ridden me your whole life, and I've always done whatever you asked. Do you think I want to hurt you?"

Balaam was embarrassed about how he had treated his donkey. "Oh, sorry."

At that exact moment, God opened Balaam's eyes and he saw what the donkey saw—a glorious angel standing in the middle of the road with a massive sword in his hand.

When the sorcerer saw the angel, he fell right on his face.

"Balaam, why did you strike your donkey like that?" the angel asked. "I came to stop you because you only want money. If your donkey had not saved you, you'd be dead right now!"

Balaam begged, "I'm sorry! I sinned! If you want, I can turn around this minute and head home."

The angel replied, "You can still go, but make sure that you only say the words that God tells you to say."

So Balaam continued on his way with the leaders of Moab.

King Balak was so excited to see Balaam that he ran out to meet him on the road. "Finally! What took you so long?" Balak asked.

"Don't worry about it," Balaam nervously replied. "I'm here now. But I'm warning you, I can only speak the words that Israel's God tells me to, ok?"

What do you think God will have Balaam say? Will He punish Israel for all their sins? Will He curse them for their disobedience?

BALAAM SPEAKS GOD'S WORDS

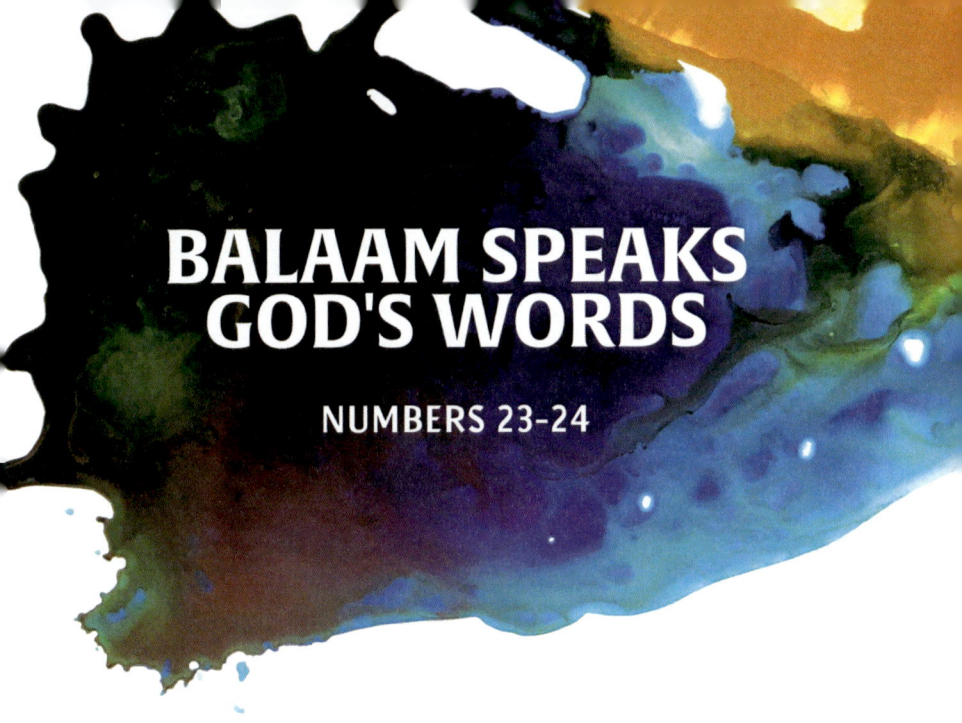

NUMBERS 23-24

King Balak could hardly contain his excitement. Today was finally the day that Balaam would curse those nasty Israelites. The king hurried to Balaam's room. "Rise and shine! Time to show those Israelites who's boss!"

Balak and his sorcerer journeyed to a place called Bamoth-baal, a mountain where Balaam could clearly see the Israelite's camp in the distance.

Balak and all the leaders of Moab built altars and offered sacrifices to try to trick the LORD into turning on His people. That couldn't possibly work…could it?!

But Balaam went by himself to see if the God of Israel would speak to him. He told the king, "If their God talks to me, I'll come back and tell you exactly what He says."

Balak trembled with anticipation, ready to run these wandering scoundrels right off the map. Finally, Balaam returned, looked at the camp of Israel, and spoke.

> "From Aram, Balak has brought me,
>   A curse on Israel to speak.
> But how can I talk poorly
>   Of a people so unique?
> These people, God has blessed them.
>   Their numbers fill the land.
> I'd rather join than curse them!
>   To be like them would be grand!"

"What did you just do?!" Balak was boiling with anger. "I brought you here for one job—to curse my enemies, and you've done nothing but bless them!"

Balaam shrugged, "I told you I could only say what their God would let me."

"Fine, fine, fine." The king shook his head. "Come with me to the top of Mount Pisgah where you can still see them and give it another try. This time do it right!"

So, they all climbed another mountain, offered more sacrifices, and let the sorcerer talk to Israel's God. Soon, Balaam was ready with more words from the LORD.

> "The God of Israel is true.
>   He does not change or lie.
> The things He says He'll surely do,
>   Never will He deny.
> You can gather every wizard,
>   They can call forth every spell,
> But if God has said He'll bless them,
>   His people will always do well.
> God brought them out of Egypt,
>   His rescue of them is complete.
> They'll live in the Land of Promise,
>   With the bad guys in defeat."

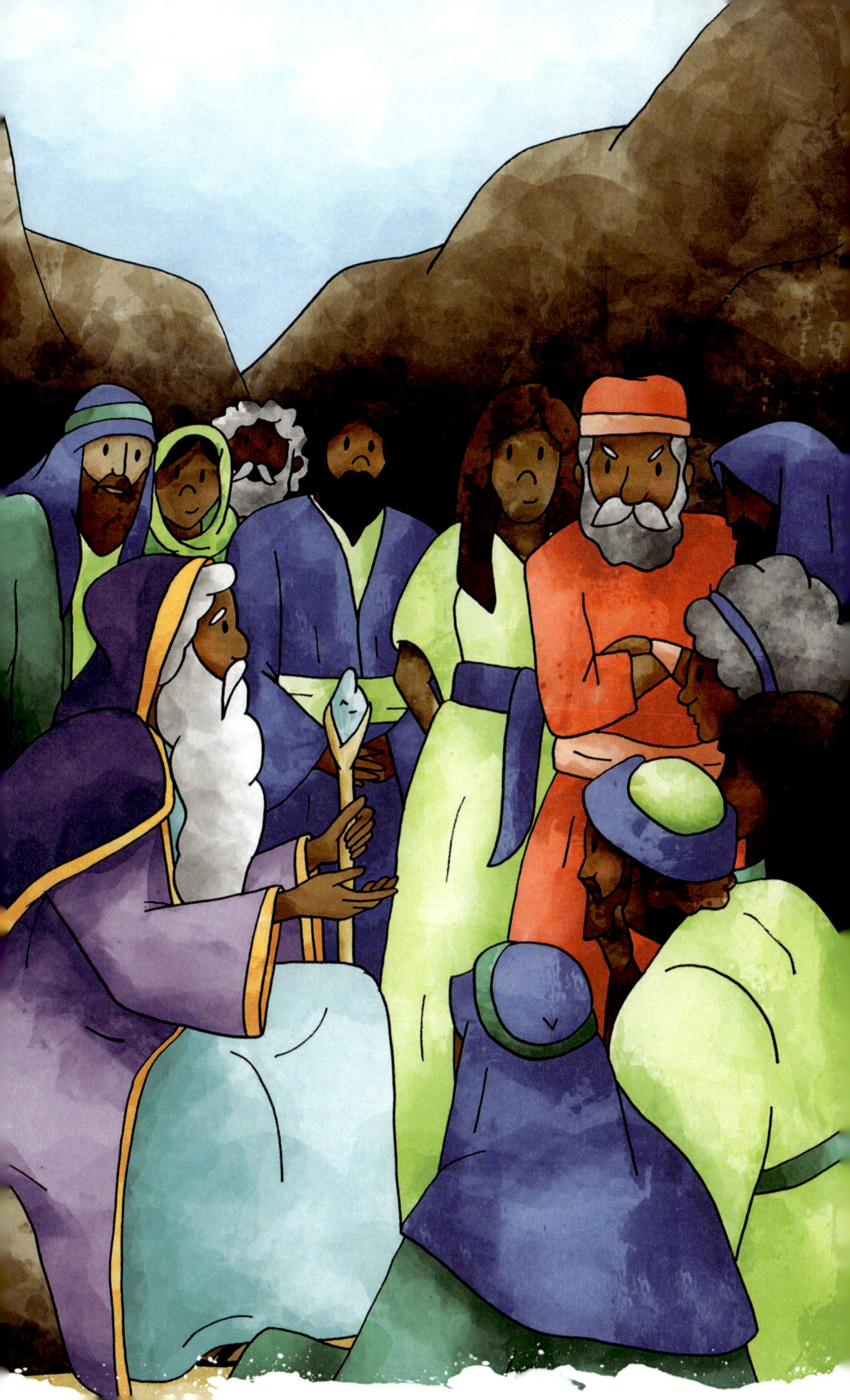

"Stop it! I don't want you to curse them anymore—because you just keep blessing them instead!" the king roared.

"Look, I keep telling you that God was the one who would put the words in my mouth," Balaam replied.

"OK, you get one last chance, Balaam. Let's go to the top of Mount Peor and give it one final shot."

So, they packed up and headed to a new mountain, made more altars, offered more sacrifices, and Balaam spoke to God one last time.

When he came back, he said:

> "The words of a man who sees clearly,
> For God has opened my eyes:
> God's people, they live in rich beauty.
> Their gardens and trees reach the skies.
> Their rivers of water flow freely.
> Their kingdom will rule over all.
> Their enemies all will lie beaten.
> Those cursing them one day will fall."

King Balak clapped his hands together in fury. "That does it! Get out of here! You didn't just fail to curse Israel—you actually blessed them three times! I told you to speak bad words over them, and you have only said good word after good word!"

Balaam reminded the king, "From the very beginning, I told you that even for a whole house filled with silver and gold, I couldn't say a single word that the LORD did not give me. Now, before I leave, let me tell you one last thing that God has shown me about the future of His people."

Balaam turned again to look over the camp of Israel.

"With these eyes that God has now opened
    I see Someone appear far away.
He'll shine like a star in the heavens,
    And He'll rule like a King in His day.
He'll crush the head of His rival,
    He'll cause every evil to cease.
He'll rescue the lives of His people,
    And He'll guide every nation in peace."

Balaam's benedictions, the good words from God that he spoke over Israel, show us that God never deserts His people—not even when they sin.

In fact, God reminded His children that He would one day send Someone to save those sinful people. Someone who would shower them with love and forgiveness. Someone who would defeat all of their enemies. Someone who would not only lead them into a beautiful land but would lead them into the presence of God forever. Not a theophany, but the real God Himself.

We know this "Someone" is Jesus. Jesus, the Son of God, came to earth as a human, obeyed His Father in every way, defeated sin and Satan when He died on the cross, conquered death when He rose from the grave, and won, for us, eternal life with God forever.

What a breathtaking, incredible God!

OLD SIN & NEW BEGINNINGS

NUMBERS 25-27

After hearing all the good things Balaam said about God's people, you'd probably think he was a good guy, huh? Well, guess again!

You see, Balaam sent some women to Israel to tempt God's people to worship a false god named Baal. As Balaam stood on the top of the mountain speaking God's blessing over His people, some Israelites were at the bottom of the mountain bowing down to imaginary gods!

The LORD, of course, was angry with these Israelites who turned from Him to follow Baal. He had only been kind to them, but they hated Him in return.

So, He sent another plague to punish them, just like one of the plagues in Egypt. The obedient Israelites were angry too—so angry they started a civil war against the Israelites who worshipped Baal! Many of the Israelites who hated God died, but the plague and the war finally ended.

After it was over, God told Moses, "The time is almost here. Your punishment of wandering in the desert for 40 long years is nearly over. Many of the people who refused to believe in Me have died. Count every man who can fight in a war—20 years old and older." So, Moses gathered the people and counted them just like before.

From Reuben's tribe: 43,730 men.
From Simeon's tribe: 22,200 men.
From Gad's tribe: 40,500 men.
From Judah's tribe: 76,500 men.
From Issachar's tribe: 64,300 men.
From Zebulun's tribe: 60,500 men.
From Manasseh's tribe: 52,700 men.
From Ephraim's tribe: 32,500 men.
From Benjamin's tribe: 45,600 men.
From Dan's tribe: 64,400 men.
From Asher's tribe: 53,400 men.
From Naphtali's tribe: 45,400 men.

And the grand total: 601,730 men who could fight in a war!

"Remember these numbers when you get to the Promised Land—they will help you decide who can live where," God told Moses. "For a big family, give them a lot of room to spread out. A small family won't need as much space, of course."

Then Moses counted the Levites—that special tribe who served in the temple. He counted all of the boys and men, no matter how young. There were 23,000 of them!

But, the Levites wouldn't get their own land. They'd live in special cities throughout the Promised Land, so they could live with the different tribes and teach them about God.

Then God reminded Moses, "As for all those Israelites who believed the scaredy-cat spies and refused to go into the Promised Land the first time—they'll continue to wander in the wilderness until they all die. After that, you can finally go home." An exciting new beginning was just around the corner for Israel!

But a sad ending was on the way as well. The LORD said to Moses, "Go up to the mountain called Abarim. From there, you'll be able to see the land I'm giving to Israel. After you see it, I'll bring you to be with Me. You won't be able to go with the people because you sinned against Me when you hit the rock with your staff to make water come out at Meribah."

Moses sadly nodded, then asked, "God, will you give the people a new leader who can guide them? Otherwise, they'll wander around like lost sheep."

God agreed and said, "Go get Joshua, the son of Nun. He was one of the faithful spies who trusted Me. My Spirit is in him so he can lead. Lay your hand on him in front of all the people. They will know that they need to listen to him now just like they listened to you."

So, Moses told the people of Israel that Joshua would be their new leader—the one who would lead them back home, to the land promised to Abraham so many years ago.

A TASTE OF THE FUTURE

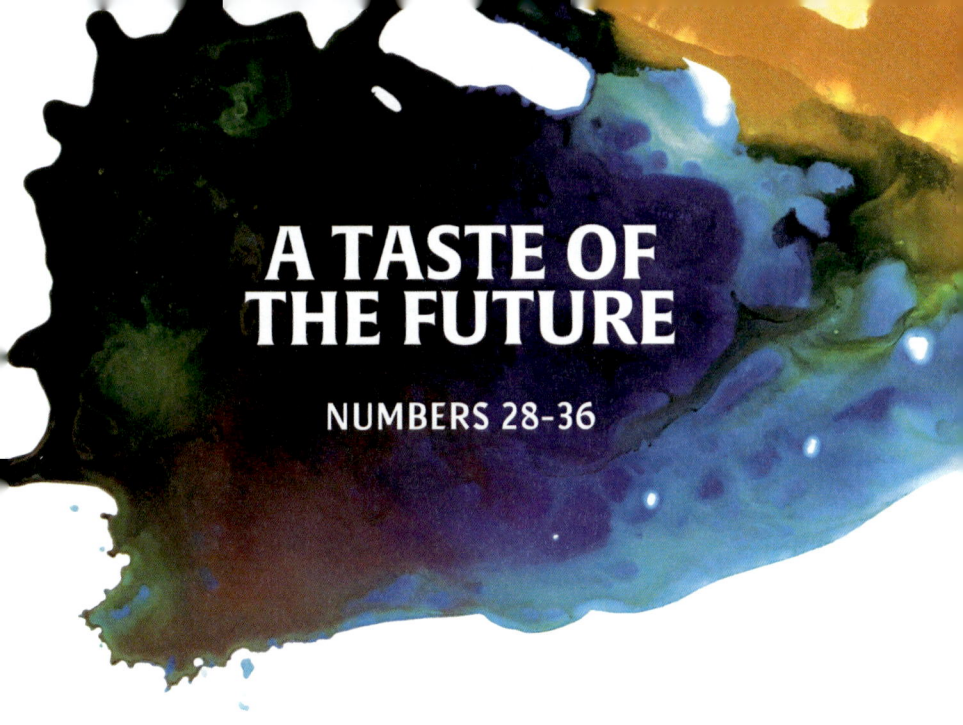

NUMBERS 28-36

Have you ever been in the kitchen while someone was baking a cake? Every once in a while, they might let you have a lick of the icing while the cake is still in the oven. Even though you must wait until the cake is finished before you can gobble it up, you get a little taste of how delicious it will be when it's done.

That's what the end of the book of Numbers is like for the people of Israel. They were still not in the Promised Land, but were getting closer and closer every hour! God was excited to fulfill His promises, and He wanted to give His people a delicious taste of what was to come.

The first taste of the future was a bit surprising. It was a great battle! Do you remember King Balak and Balaam, the sorcerer? Well, since they tempted God's people to worship Baal and tried to curse them, God planned to punish them. So, He told Moses, "Go to war with the Midianites—the people of Balak and Balaam. After that, your job will be done, and you can come to be with Me."

Moses gathered the army of Israel—12,000 of their best fighters—and went to war. Israel fought and fought until there were no enemies left.

The most shocking thing was that not a single Israelite soldier was even hurt in the battle! They were safe because God was fighting for them! The Israelites ended up with tons of gold and silver, cows, sheep, and donkeys after they defeated the people of Balak and Balaam.

God told the Israelites, "Make sure to fight just like this once you cross the river into the Promised Land. If you leave any of your enemies, they will tempt you to worship false gods. They'll be more annoying than a pointy rock in your sandal!

"Also, the way you divided up all your stuff—that's how you need to divide up the land so that everyone has just what they need." The Israelites grew braver and braver after getting to see how God would fight their battles against their enemies.

The second taste of the future that God gave the Israelites was a taste of home. Once the battle was over, three of the tribes—well, two and a half of them—Gad, Reuben, and half of Manasseh—loved the land of the Midianites so much that they wanted to make it their home.

But this made some Israelites nervous. "Wait, if you make your home here, you won't cross the river with us into the Promised Land. You'll forget about us. You might even forget God!"

"No way!" replied the two and a half tribes. "We will make a home for our wives and our children, but we will send our fighting men with you over the river. We want to obey God and help our friends! Then, after we've fought all God's enemies, we'll come back home to our families." This made everyone feel a lot better knowing their friends weren't doubting God again. And it was exciting to see God already keeping His promise to give them a home!

The third taste of the future God gave the Israelites was... you guessed it...more rules! But these weren't just any old rules. They were rules for when Israel finally moved into the Promised Land. Most of the rules were about the sacrifices they would offer for forgiveness from God. Those are pretty important, right?

Plus, they were fun rules too—do you remember the huge, gigantic, unbelievable party that God commanded the Israelites to celebrate when they consecrated the tabernacle?

Well, when the people finally made their homes in Canaan, God commanded them to have five parties every year! Five! They even got to have a mini-party every week!

When they had these parties, God's people were to offer lots of sacrifices to remember how bad their sin was, but even more to remember God's goodness—how He forgives those sins, how He saved them from Egypt, and how He protected and provided for them in the desert. Those are all good reasons to throw a party, don't you think?

What a long, wild journey! Let's take a walk down memory lane as Numbers comes to a close.

Remember way back—all those years earlier, God rescued Israel out of slavery. He defeated the Egyptians with plagues and showed that the true God of Israel was more powerful than all the false gods of Egypt. He protected Israel with the blood of the lamb during Passover.

The next day, Israel marched and danced right out of Egypt toward their Promised Land with Moses and Aaron guiding the way! God parted the Red Sea, and His people walked through on dry land. They followed God's special cloud. He gave them water to drink and bread from heaven to eat.

But Israel was tempted and disobeyed God over and over. God punished them for not trusting Him, and they wandered in the desert for 40 years. When he was 123 years old, their beloved leader Aaron died on Mount Hor.

The Israelites fought battles against enemies and won because God was with them. The entire journey, God showed His character—a good Father who protected and provided for His children, but who would also punish His children for disobeying since He knew how destructive disobedience can be. Through it all, God kept His promises and led His people every step of the way.

Moses stood before God's people to remind them of this story. After Moses finished speaking, Joshua, God's next leader for Israel, came to stand beside him. Remembering God's faithfulness, the people turned their eyes to the distance—to the walls of Jericho, the entrance to the Promised Land.

LAST WORDS: JESUS DEFEATS TEMPTATION

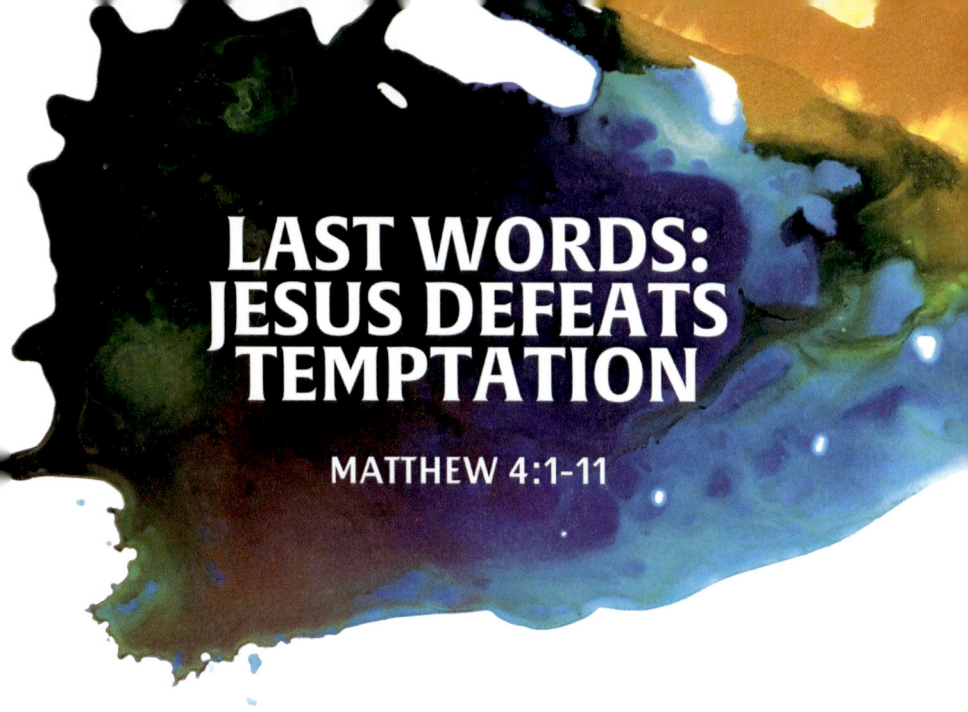

MATTHEW 4:1–11

After the book of Numbers, things didn't get much better for the Israelites. Sure, they finally entered the Promised Land because God fought off their enemies for them. But the Israelites were not obedient and did not get rid of all their enemies, and—just like God told them they would—they began to worship false gods. God warned them and punished them, but He was also patient. He even made more promises to Israel and gave them a powerful king named David.

But the Israelites refused to listen to their God—no matter how numerous the warnings. So, God sent mighty armies to fight the Israelites.

Soon, the Israelites were taken as prisoners out of the Promised Land because of their disobedience. After 70 years, God brought them back, but it was just never the same.

In the middle of their sin and sadness, though, God told them of a Savior—a Messiah, God Himself—who would come and rescue them again. Just like Moses rescued them from slavery in Egypt...only better, because this new Moses would rescue them from their slavery to sin.

Over 1,000 years after Numbers, that Savior was born. It was Jesus, of course—the Son of God who would finally, fully, and perfectly rescue His people. After He grew up, Jesus began to show and tell everyone how He planned to save the world. It all started with water, similar to how Israel began their journey by passing through the Red Sea. Jesus was baptized with water by a man you may have heard of, John the Baptist. Then, like Israel, Jesus headed to the wilderness.

Just as Israel spent 40 years in the desert, Jesus spent 40 days and 40 nights in the wilderness. But Jesus didn't eat a single thing the whole time! I bet His stomach growled so loud, they could hear it all the way back in town!

While Jesus was hungry, Satan slithered over to tempt Him, just as he tempted Adam and Eve in the garden. "Jesus, if You really are who You say You are—the Son of God Himself—then turn these stones into bread. I know You're hungry. You'll get to eat and prove me wrong!"

Being hungry makes obedience hard. Remember how the Israelites complained all the time about food and water? And they were never even without food like Jesus was! But unlike Israel, Jesus was faithful to His Father.

"No! The Bible teaches that people don't live by bread alone," Jesus told Satan. "God's words are more delicious and filling than the richest of foods."

Satan wasn't ready to give up yet, though. He brought Jesus to the top of the temple (which was like the tabernacle) and said, "Ok, Jesus. I'll give You another shot to prove You really are God's Son. Leap off the top of the temple. If God loves You, surely He won't let You get hurt! Even the Bible says 'God will protect You with His angels. They'll keep You from even stubbing Your toe on a rock!'"

Satan wanted Jesus to prove that God was really on His side. That's a difficult thing to believe sometimes, especially when it feels like God is nowhere to be found. The Israelites felt this way a lot during the book of Numbers. They constantly argued with one another about whether or not God really loved them and would keep all of His promises.

But Jesus didn't doubt. No way! He knew His Father was with Him, even though He couldn't see Him. "Satan, the Bible also says not to test the LORD your God. I already trust Him! I don't have to prove it to the likes of you."

Now Satan was frustrated. He wanted to trap Jesus because he knew Jesus had come to save the world. If Satan could make Jesus sin here in the desert, Jesus would fail His rescue mission before it even started!

Then, like a light bulb flipping on, Satan had one last idea. "Jesus, You want to be the King of the world, right? Well, I promise that if You bow down and worship me, I'll give You every single inch of this world for Your kingdom!"

Jesus would never bow down to Satan, would He? But wait...the Israelites, God's people, sinned by worshipping false gods in the wilderness. The true God wasn't doing what they wanted, so they found pretend gods they thought they could boss around to get what they wanted. That was the worst sin of all and the hardest temptation to fight.

But Jesus didn't even think about giving in to Satan—not for a second! "Get out of here, Satan! The Bible commands us to worship the LORD our God alone! He's the only real God. And He's the only God who will always love and protect His people! You can't fool me!" And with that, Satan dashed away from Jesus like the slimy snake he was.

You see, Jesus was like Israel in one Person—only far better. Unlike Israel, Jesus always obeyed the voice of His Father. When He was in the desert, He never sinned. In fact, He never sinned even once in His whole life! He always loved and cared for those around Him. He was never selfish. He trusted His Father even in the hardest moments.

Since Jesus obeyed His Father all the time, He was like a perfect, spotless lamb sacrificed to forgive people of their sins.

When Jesus went to the cross, an amazing miracle happened. All the sins of God's people—including yours and mine—were placed on Jesus like a heavy backpack full of thousands of rocks. Even though our sin weighed Him down, Jesus never got off the cross. He was lifted high for all to see (like the snake statue in the desert) so that everyone who believes in Him would be saved.

Not only did all of our sin fall on Jesus, but all of Jesus' goodness and obedience is placed on us when we believe—like a royal robe and a glittering crown.

When God looks at us, He doesn't see our sin. He sees Jesus' goodness and righteousness, which He gave to us!

The Israelites did not deserve God's faithfulness and forgiveness. Because of our sin, we don't deserve God's faithfulness and forgiveness either. But Jesus gives forgiveness to us. And even though it cost Him His life, His forgiveness costs us nothing at all.

Now, just as Jesus rose from the dead after the cross, we can know that if we believe in Him, we will rise from the dead to live with Him forever—in the new heavens and the new earth. Our new and better Promised Land.